PÁDRAIG McC

A WEDDING OF YOUR OWN

Cer
D.

VERITAS

First published 1978 by
Veritas Publications
7/8 Lower Abbey Street
Dublin 1
Ireland
Email publications@veritas.ie
Website www.veritas.ie

2nd edition published 1984
3rd edition published 1988
This edition first published 2003

ISBN 1 85390 678 6

A catalogue record for this book is available from the British Library.

Concordat cum originali: ✠ Desmond Connell, Archbishop of Dublin
Nihil Obstat: ✠ Richard Sherry DD
Imprimi Potest: ✠ Desmond Connell

Acknowledgments
Excerpts from the English translation of the *Roman Missal* © 1973, International Committee on English in the Liturgy (ICEL), Inc. All rights reserved. The text of the Marriage Rite, as adapted by the Liturgical Commission of the Irish Hierarchy in consultation with the International Committee on English in the Liturgy and approved by the Irish Episcopal Conference and the Sacred Congregation for Divine Worship, together with the Pastoral notes, is copyright © 1970, 1980 ✠ Tomás Ó Muiris, Institiúid Chumarsáide Chaitliceach na hÉireann.

The Psalms quoted are from *The Psalms: A New Translation* published by William Collins Sons & Co. Ltd and are used by permission of The Grail.

Scripture quotations are from the *New Jerusalem Bible* published and © 1966, 1967 and 1968 by Darton, Longman & Todd Ltd and Doubleday & Co. Inc. and are used by permission of the publishers.

Cover design by Bill Bolger
Illustrations by Marketgraphics
Printed in the Republic of Ireland by Betaprint Ltd, Dublin
Veritas books are printed on paper made from the wood pulp of managed forests. For every tree felled, at least one tree is planted, thereby renewing natural resources.

We

---

and

---

in view of our marriage on

---

at the Church of

---

before

---

and

---

as witnesses, and before

---

as officiating celebrant,

declare that, with God's help, we shall:

Remain steadfast in our love for one another and in our faith in Jesus Christ, the Son of God;
Open our marriage to be guided by the spirit of love;
Live our marriage as active members of the Church, the Body of Christ;
Guard against everything that might weaken our faith;
Do all in our power to share the riches of our faith with all children who may be born of our marriage;

And we call on our Church to strengthen us in good times and in bad; we call on our friends to witness what we do today and to support us with loving prayer.
As husband and wife, with the Church, may we grow in unity;
So that, together, we may give glory to God now and forever.

CONTENTS

Appendices 245

WELCOME TO THE FEAST!

There's a feast of good things to choose from in arranging a wedding ceremony. This book is like a menu for the feast. My job is like that of the waiter: to let you know what you can choose from the riches of the store-house in the tradition of a Catholic wedding. As with many menus, there may be some items you are not familiar with, so I've just tried to add words to explain them, so that you will be better able to make your choices.

There are many books and resources (computer programs, internet, etc.) available on the subject of planning for a wedding, which deal with matters like cakes, car hire, photography, hotels, honeymoons, home-buying, legal matters, clothes, what you can expect the best man or bridesmaid to do, and so on. This book, on the other hand, deals with the heart of the wedding day: the celebration itself, where the couple give their promise to love one another as husband and wife. The 'menu' consists of the elements that may be chosen for the celebration, in accordance with the practice of the Catholic Church in Ireland.

This book is largely addressed to couples preparing for their wedding. Apart from being like a menu for the celebration, the book might also serve as a conversation-starter between the prospective bride and groom. I hope that many others may also find it a useful store-house. If you are already married, you may find some material here to help you reflect on your experience, or to plan for an anniversary. If you are a minister of the Church involved in wedding celebrations, this book may help you in putting your experience at the service of couples planning their wedding celebration.

If you are planning your own wedding, it's advisable not to leave it until the last month or two. Starting your preparations six months ahead will allow you to take your time over it and give you a chance to change your choices if you want to. Try not to leave it to just one of you to make all the decisions about the celebration.

Just as you wouldn't order everything on a restaurant menu, likewise you won't use everything in this book! There are choices to be made. You may be inclined to go straight to the readings and prayers and words of consent – and that's fine. But if you take the time to go to the section 'Introducing Christian Marriage' on page 31 and talk together about each of the parts there, you may find that you'll get a lot more out of the different choices you can make for your wedding celebration. You may feel that 'Christian marriage' is no different to any other marriage, except that it starts with a church celebration. See if that section makes a difference. Don't feel you have to agree with everything there just because it's in the book. Equally, don't disagree with what's there just because it may annoy you or challenge you!

Behind everything in this book is the purpose of seeing how tremendous and wonderful a gift Christian marriage is. The wedding of Christians is not about one day; it's about the beginning of a process: the wedding of two lifetimes – and more. How do you imagine heaven? The reading on page 151 from the Book of Revelation describes heaven as being like a wedding feast: the 'wedding' celebration of the 'Lamb' (Jesus Christ) and the 'bride' (the people of God) in everlasting faithfulness and love and life. May your wedding day bring you, and everyone with you, a taste of that! As that reading says: '*Blessed are those who are invited to the wedding feast of the Lamb*'.

TO THE BRIDE AND GROOM

I have great pleasure in inviting you to the feast described in this book! (Of course, I must confess that I'm not the one who provides all the things on the menu; these have come to us over thousands of years, and are still good today, even without a freezer.) It's my privilege to be able to put it before you.

In the year 2000, there were 19,168 marriages registered in the Republic of Ireland. A lot of weddings for a small country! No matter how many there may be, each one is personal to the two people involved. There's something so personal about a wedding that I wanted to call this book *A Wedding of Your Own:* but there's so much more in it than that. This book can't make it a wedding of your own; it's simply an invitation for *you* to make it *yours*. Yours, because it is so personal, a matter for you both. Yours, because it is a gift from God to you that you're about to celebrate. Yours, because it is your personal gift to God and to his people and to his world.

What can a book, or any person, say about your marriage? There is a saying attributed to the Chinese teacher, Lao-tzu:

> *Those who know do not say;*
> *those who say do not know.*

Fr Tony de Mello tells of students discussing this. When their teacher came in, they asked him what it meant. He said: 'Which of you knows the fragrance of a rose?' All the students indicated that they knew. The teacher said: 'Put it into words'. All of them were silent.

So much of what marriage, and Christian marriage, means is beyond words. We use actions and symbols that go beyond words. If you could say what a kiss means, why not just say it, and not bother to kiss? However well you might say what a kiss means, the action says, and does, more. Words can say a lot, but words will never express the full depth of meaning; they can help point further. In a wedding celebration we use words, but we also use actions and symbols: rings, holding hands, flowers, gathering friends and family, clothes, sharing food – make your own list.

This book has many words. They will never tell the full story. But if the words can help you find ways to express your life-experience, and your faith in one another and in God, then they can help you plan your wedding so that the words and actions and symbols will speak more eloquently. That is one reason why I suggest that this book may serve as a 'conversation-starter'. I have my own experience to draw on, including many years as a priest, and the experience of many people who have honoured me with their confidence and their love. But if you listen only to me, and not to your own life-experience, you're leaving out a vital ingredient. The value of the book is in how you, the readers, use it to 'interact with one another'. That, by the way, is the original meaning of the word 'intercourse'!

Part of your mind and heart may feel that what I say is too unreal. And it will be, if it just remains 'out there'. Instead, let the things I say here about marriage for Christians take flesh in you whatever way you can. Even if they sound impossible, just imagine what it would be like if they were true. Let yourself taste them, and see if you discover something for yourself. You may discover in a new way that this idea of Christian marriage is no more ridiculous than believing in a God who is totally *love.*

Yours is a wedding that will last not just a wedding day, but will continue all the days of your life. A wedding of a lifetime. A wedding where two lifetimes continue to become one. Marriage is not a fixed thing, a 'state' like a statue or a house; it's more like a continuous process, like the life of a person. A marriage enriches not just the husband and wife, but the rest of our human family, both single and married. A couple who continue to 'wed', to 'marry', are a living sign of the power of love through thick and thin; a sign that love can unite even where everything seems to cause division; a living 'sacrament'; a sign and embodiment of the love that God has given us in Jesus.

It's as if the Father said to Jesus: *'Will you commit yourself to this person in love, for better, for worse, for richer, for poorer, in sickness and in health, all the days of your life?'* And Jesus answers: *'I will! I will be with them all days even till the end of time!'* It's not just *your* marriage; it belongs to God too; it belongs to the Church; it belongs to the world.

Here, a first question to consider is whether a church wedding is really what you want. It may seem a strange question to ask – after all, you did pick up this book! When you have read and talked together about what Christian marriage is (as explained in the section, 'Introducing Christian Marriage'), you can decide whether this is what you have in mind. Clearly, I hope a church wedding is what you will want.

It is important to know that Christian marriage is what a church wedding is about. Why would a couple want the wedding if they don't want the marriage that goes with it? Some people for whom faith in God and in Jesus Christ is not in any way a part of their lives will decide that, for them, the most genuine and sincere celebration is a non-religious wedding. Some for whom faith is not at present a part of their lives may decide, on knowing what Christian marriage is about, that this is what they really have in mind, and they may begin again to let their faith in God rekindle. If just one person of the couple lives an active faith, each person of the couple can take part in the celebration at their own level.

This book can help you plan your wedding and inform you of some of the aspects of it that you may not have thought about before. This knowledge is contained in some of what the Liturgy of the Word of God says about marriage, in the Liturgy of Marriage itself, and in the Liturgy of the Eucharist. Don't be put off by this word 'liturgy' – it's what you do each time you come to celebrate Mass, just as 'prose' is a term for the words you're speaking most of the time without remembering it's prose!

I hope you won't skip over pages 31 to 93, before we get down to the ceremony itself: I suggest you read these pages and talk them over together. In these pages, I try to offer you some of the foundation of what it means for a Christian to marry. Foundations help all that is built on them to hang together. A church wedding is not just a nice custom of having a ceremony in a church, so as to have a bit of a show. *If you're having a church wedding, have it because you want it for what it really is, not because other people have it or expect it!* Later, after you've picked out the readings and so on that you like, you might read over these same pages again, and I hope you'll get a whole new depth of meaning. And if, when you've read it, you feel you really knew it all before – that's great.

I can't say everything that getting married involves. Could anybody? It takes a lifetime to experience it, and even then, it would be hard to put just your own experience into words. The material you can choose from for your wedding offers a lot from the experience of many people over a long time. The choices you have in planning your own wedding ceremony say a lot of different things about marriage. You can choose whichever things mean most to the two of you, that you would like those who will be at the wedding to see and hear. You can have the ceremony as short as less than an hour, or as long as you feel would be good or possible. This presents you with such choices.

Some choices mean more than others. Your wedding would probably mean much the same, no matter what day or date you have it. The readings you choose and the words you use to give yourselves to one another could say a lot more about what your wedding means than the particular date you choose.

If you have a preference for a certain day, you may need to reserve the church up to a year in advance, or even earlier. That's about the time you could start planning your ceremony, with the help of the minister – normally a priest or a deacon – who would assist at your wedding. This is the person who, being present, asks the two parties to manifest their consent and in the name of the Church receives it. Where there are no priests or deacons, the diocesan bishop can delegate lay persons to assist at marriages, if the Episcopal Conference has given its prior approval and the permission of the Holy See (Rome) has been obtained. Remember, such a person who 'assists' does not 'marry' the bride and groom; the bride and groom themselves are the ones who are the 'ministers' of the sacrament to one another!

So, please take all the time you need to plan your wedding. It will mean much more to you. The parts you choose will mean a lot; the parts you read over but decide not to use will be there, too, as part of your preparation.

Even if you feel that one of you is better able to do this kind of thing than the other, please work on it together and help one another by sharing your ideas. It is equally important to both of you. You may have different ideas – it wouldn't be the last time this happens; but you discuss other things about your wedding and your marriage – the religious side deserves discussion just as much as any other side. If you grew up in a Christian environment, this is probably very deep in you, even if your faith at present is not as alive as it could be. If you feel that you can't handle the religious side of things – that's one of the reasons for this book, so that you can have a way to tackle it.

Before you go any further

If you're about to do something you've never done before, something that will affect your whole life, it is sensible to avail of whatever help is there. That is what marriage preparation is for: not to tell you how you will have to live your marriage (that is the privilege of husband and wife to decide on), but to give you the benefit of the experience of many other people so you can have a fuller picture than you might get on your own. Your marriage will be different – no two marriages are the same – but that doesn't mean you can't learn from the experience of others.

Enquire in your parish about marriage preparation well in advance, to be sure of availing of whatever there may be in your area.

This may not be high on your list of things to do while preparing for your wedding. However, it can be helpful to you in looking beyond the day of the wedding to the life that follows. It can give you extra ways of seeing and coping with situations, and can provide you with a lot to talk about. There can also be the opportunity to meet with other couples who are preparing for their wedding and married life.

Marriage preparation courses are offered by various organisations. You'll find a list of contacts on page 242. As well as informal courses, your local area may have more informal resources. Again, your parish is a good place to enquire.

The preparation you choose may teach you a lot, or very little. Whichever way, it should give you material for talking with one another about your marriage. Even if you learn little – wouldn't it be good to know that you had already discussed among yourselves whatever the course dealt with?

WHAT SHOULD WE DO FIRST?

Some matters to decide on first of all:

1. Is a church wedding what we really want?
2. If so, which church?
3. What kind of wedding ceremony?
4. When will we celebrate our wedding?
5. What are the first steps?

Do we want a church wedding?

Does it seem strange to ask this question? We would like to encourage Christians to celebrate a church wedding, of course, and I hope this book will encourage you in this. It should help you consider what a church wedding actually is. If you are clear that the Christian understanding of marriage is what you really want, even though you know that you fail in many ways, then you can make a sincere decision to plan for a church wedding. Your parish will be very happy to help you in making your plans accordingly.

On the other hand, if you know in your own heart and soul that faith in God, and being a member of the Church, do not really figure in your lives and you are not ready to let them be a part of your lives at this time, it is important that you consider waiting until you are ready, or consider a non-church wedding. On the day when you promise to love each other truly for the rest of your lives, it would be sad to have anything false about your celebration. As you look through the parts of the ceremony, you will see that you would be saying and agreeing with the whole Christian understanding of marriage. If this is not for you, you can make a sincere decision to contact your local office of the Registrar of Marriages in Ireland, or the equivalent elsewhere, and make your plans.

Which church?

Normally, the wedding takes place in the parish of the residence of the bride or of the groom. This is the 'natural' place: the parish where you belong to the community, where you come for your Sundays – a place where you have some roots.

But what happens if you 'don't have a parish', if you have been moving around and don't feel you belong anywhere? In this case, it is important for each of you to make contact with your local parish right away; and to do what you can to 'belong'. (If you move to a new home after the wedding, make sure you contact your new parish soon.) It's here that you make the first contact to arrange your wedding plans. You can get all the information you need there.

What if you don't like the church building in either of your parishes? This can happen, and the wedding can be arranged for elsewhere. But the first place to consider should be the parish, or one of the parishes, where you belong now. Couples sometimes pick on a church somewhere because of its picturesque location, or because it's near a hotel where they want to have a wedding reception – a place where they have no connection whatever. I strongly suggest that you do not base your choice of location for the wedding ceremony on how good it will be for the photographs, or for convenience for the reception afterwards. If you do plan your wedding ceremony for a parish other than your own, make sure you check whether that parish will require you to arrange for a priest to come. If you are not both members of the same Church, enquire in your parish about arrangements. In this case, you may need to allow more time.

Wedding abroad: In particular, if you are planning to celebrate your wedding abroad, you need to find out what is necessary – ask in your own parish. Persons marrying abroad should ensure that all the legal requirements of the country in question are met, and should enquire as to the procedure for obtaining a marriage certificate from that country – the relevant embassy or religious authorities may be able to advise. If a marriage certificate is in a foreign language, it should normally be accepted for official purposes in the Republic of Ireland if accompanied by an official translation or a translation from a recognised translation agency. Certificates of Freedom to marry (also known as 'Certificates de Coutume' or 'Certificates of Nulla Osta'), which state that a person is not married, may be needed for marriage in some countries. Irish citizens living in Ireland wishing to obtain such a certificate should apply to the Consular Section of the Department of Foreign Affairs, 72/76 St Stephen's Green, Dublin 2 (Tel: (01) 478 0822, extension 304). Irish citizens living abroad should contact their nearest Irish Embassy. See also the 'Contacts' section at the end of the book.

What kind of wedding ceremony?

The essential celebration of ***the wedding ceremony*** itself consists of your exchange of consent before the witnesses; this is set in the context of prayers, readings and symbolic actions (rings, etc.). Along with this, there may be music and other elements you choose.

The wedding ceremony ***can also be celebrated in the context of the celebration of Mass***. Here, in addition to the above, we prepare the altar with bread and wine, we pray the 'Eucharistic Prayer' where we give thanks to God, remembering in particular what Jesus did at the supper table the night before he died, and we share in the Bread of Life in Holy Communion, a sign that we are united in Christ. From the time of the early Christians, they saw a connection between the self-giving in love of Jesus, and the self-giving in love of husband and wife. Which way you choose will depend on your own situation and circumstances. If in doubt, discuss it with one of the staff of your parish, or with the priest or other minister who will be involved in the ceremony.

When will we celebrate our wedding?

First of all, you will need to allow enough time for what needs to be done before you marry. In Ireland, each of you needs to contact your home parish at least three months before the date you choose. If you are not members of the same Church, be sure to allow extra time for arranging it.

In addition, in the Republic of Ireland, you must give at least three months' notice to the local Registrar of Marriages for the place where you want to celebrate your wedding. This is civil law; it is quite simple and has nothing to do with your church, except that we may not go ahead with the wedding without this! Enquire locally about who to contact. The minimum age at which a person, ordinarily resident in the Republic of Ireland, may contract a marriage valid in Irish law is eighteen years of age, whether the marriage takes place in Ireland or elsewhere. Outside the Republic of Ireland, check what civil requirements may be.

To decide on a day, you'll need to check with the parish where you hope to celebrate your wedding. For example, in many places, weddings are not celebrated on Sundays or Holy Days. If you are thinking of late March or anytime in April, check the date of Easter for that year. You'll find a list of Easter dates in Appendix 6. Holy Week – the week before Easter Sunday – is not a good time. Because of the season of Lent, the weeks from Ash Wednesday to Easter are not the most appropriate time. You will also need to be sure that the church is available for the day and time you have in mind, and that the priest or whoever will assist you at the wedding is available.

What are the first steps?

If you contact one of the staff of your own parish, they will usually be able to give you good information about taking it from there.

COUNTDOWN

How about a plan? It can be useful to have an idea of when you want to have done the many bits and pieces that go into preparing for your wedding. The following is a suggestion for a 'countdown' to your launch! Make out your own. Agree together about how you'll need to tailor it to your own situation, or make your own plan and build in the arrangements for various other things you want to do.

When?	**What we want to do**
12 months or more	Contact parish to arrange date, church, priest or other minister, and to check about the paperwork needed. Ask about preparation course, and make booking if necessary. In the case of interchurch or interfaith marriage, or any unusual factor, ask about these. If you have not done so, discuss between yourselves what part your faith in God takes in your life, and whether there are implications for your practice and lifestyle. Are there hurts, bitterness, anger, etc. that you might be able to take steps to heal? Obstacles to

your love for one another or for God? Matters to ask forgiveness for? Sources of resentment?
Each evening from now to the wedding, look back over the day and ask yourself:

a. How has love touched my life today? In your own words, say a prayer of thanks for this.
b. How have I been able to show love today? In your own words, say a prayer of thanks for this.
c. Have I failed to show love in some way today? How can I learn from this for tomorrow? In your own words, ask God's forgiveness, and say a prayer of thanks for the gift of forgiveness.

If you practise becoming aware of the ways you fail, it will help clear the path for growing in love. And any time you fail in a big way, it will be easier to face it and to deal with it.

6 months	Contact parish for appointment for completion of forms, etc. Notify civil registrar. Begin looking at what you may choose for the ceremony. If you have not done so: pray together sometimes! How about a one-day or weekend 'retreat' together for those preparing for marriage? Your parish may be able to suggest what's available.
3 months	Have a good idea of what you would like for the ceremony, and discuss it with the priest or minister assisting you. Review music for the celebration. In sending invitations, be sure to invite your guests to the wedding celebration in the church.
2 months	With the plan for the ceremony fairly well finalised, arrange with your guests about taking active part in the celebration.

	Arrange a day for a wedding rehearsal. Where music for the congregation may be unfamiliar to some, is there some way you can help them to become familiar with it in the coming weeks?
1 month	Getting hectic? Make sure you have some relaxed time together over the month. Make sure those who will read at the ceremony have copies. Keep a spare copy yourselves in case they lose theirs. You may find people telling you jokes about marriage which are decidedly 'off-colour', or making negative remarks ('Last days of freedom!' etc.) which, while intended to be humorous, are degrading to the important step you are about to make. Negative humour can be hurtful and destructive of love. Let them know gently that this is not what you need – even if they accuse you of lacking a sense of humour!
3 weeks	Go over the wedding ceremony together bit by bit. Talk about all you have chosen – what the readings, the prayers, the 'non-verbal' parts, the setting, etc., mean to you at this stage. Speak aloud to one another the words of consent you will use. Speak these words again a number of times over the coming weeks, so that you'll be very much at ease with them on the wedding day.
2 weeks	Still making sure you have some time for a prayer each day, individually and together? It will help make your wedding ceremony more meaningful. If there are pre-wedding parties:

For those who take alcohol or nicotine or any 'social stimulants' – decide now to go easy on these, even if people put pressure on you with the best of intentions. Say how you appreciate it, and still say 'No, thank you'. Set your limits, and stick to them. However pleasant they may be at the time, you know what the effects can be. You don't want to spend the weeks before your wedding day in a haze. What better stimulant could you want than the person you want to marry?

10 days

As you prepare for a whole new life together as husband and wife:
For either of you, are there matters in your past that you want to put behind you? Start this new stage of the rest of your life with a 'clean slate'?
Perhaps you could decide on when and where and with whom you could celebrate the gift of God's forgiveness in Confession: the 'Sacrament of Reconciliation'. Even if it has been a long time, there's no need to be afraid.
Remember some of the stories of Jesus: perhaps read 'The Prodigal Son' in St Luke's Gospel, chapter 15 (if you like, think of mother/daughter as well as father/son). Or the woman brought to Jesus (St John's Gospel, the beginning of chapter 8), when Jesus said: 'Has no-one condemned you? Neither do I'. And pray for one another in this!

1 week

Make sure you have all the things you need for the wedding celebration: rings; exchange of gifts if relevant; wedding candle(s) if relevant; booklet or leaflet for the ceremony if relevant; envelopes with the various offerings, and who is to look after them. You're preparing for a feast. Go easy on food in the days before it, so you'll appreciate it better. Even decide on a day of some fasting for the day before?

3 days

Remember:
It's unusual that absolutely everything goes according to plan – but that's okay. Some things that happen make a wedding day all the more memorable!
Even if something goes badly wrong, remember that you can still celebrate a perfectly good wedding.
What's needed is a man and woman:

a. who know what they are doing;
b. who intend to make this life-long commitment;
c. who are capable of carrying this out, day by day; and
d. who freely make this commitment before their witnesses.

Now relax, knowing that the Lord is with you!

TO THE MINISTER WHO OFFICIATES

Like a marriage, or the priesthood, a book such as this is always a work in progress. You may not necessarily agree with all I have written here, but I hope the book will still be of assistance to you.

This new edition is overdue. Revisions of the Rite of Marriage are in the process of moving through the various channels of Rome and ICEL (International Committee on English in the Liturgy). It is uncertain as to when further material may be available. In this edition, there are five extra readings: Proverbs 31; Romans 15; Ephesians 4; Philippians 4; and Hebrews 13. I have tried to revise the editorial material to reflect our contemporary situation in the world, and in Ireland in particular. We have come a long way from a time when people were rarely, if ever, involved in the preparation of liturgy. The social and religious environment has changed greatly since the first edition in 1978.

We continue to use the official rite for Ireland, *The Celebration of Marriage – Gnás an Phósta*, published by Veritas in 1980. The Introduction and Pastoral Notes (pages 1-10) are still worth reading. The purpose of this book is to make the riches of the Rite easily accessible to couples preparing for their wedding, so that they can do so creatively, within the Christian tradition of our Church. In order to do this, it will help if they (and we) appreciate that their love for one another right now is in some way an experience of God, who is love. In this context, the wedding day – the celebration in the church and everything else about the day – will be a significant moment in their lives as Christians, as well as on a human level. Even with a couple not much in contact with Church life, to focus on how their love changes their lives, and to see this as a reflection of how the love that God gives us in Jesus Christ can change our lives, may give them a new dimension they have never before considered. Much of what I have written here is intended to help bring this into focus. There are many other publications and resources that offer material for this.

The earlier editions of this book have shown that this material can also be useful for married people in reflecting on the gift of the sacrament of marriage, helping them to see their life together as an ongoing 'wedding', a being and becoming one, as a living sign of the unity for which Jesus prayed. It can also be useful for people who simply want to know where Christian marriage is in our faith and in our practice. *'Lex orandi, lex credendi'* – the way we worship tells what our faith is.

When this book is being used by an engaged couple to plan their wedding, they will need you to work on it with them, because you will be so closely involved with them in the ceremony. You may be aware of some feelings of *'they're taking over my job!'* – to be aware of it can help you avoid acting on it, and will help you work with them in partnership on this task which is their right and responsibility.

Some couples will be only too delighted to be fully involved. Others may be shy or reluctant: it's a whole new experience for many to be involved in planning liturgy. One or both may feel inadequate to take part in the planning; or they may feel their faith is weak or non-existent; or may simply have a less developed reading ability. You are in a position to help all couples by your love for them, even if some things requested at times may not be suitable or practicable. You can encourage them to look at the options, not just those in this book, but others too of which you may know; you can encourage them to make their own choices; and you can respect those choices, while guiding where necessary. Those of us who are 'professionals' in these areas can be tempted to step in and take over. As long as what they say is consistent with good liturgy, ask yourself 'Why not do as they suggest?'

The *Constitution on the Liturgy* of the Second Vatican Council states in section 59: 'They [the sacraments] not only presuppose faith but by words and objects they also nourish, strengthen, and express it ... the very act of celebrating them disposes the faithful most effectively to receive this grace in a fruitful manner, to worship God duly, and to practise charity. It is therefore of capital importance that the faithful easily understand the sacramental signs'. What better chance has a couple of coming closer to this, than when they are personally involved in their own wedding ceremony?

It does take more time than doing it all yourself on the day. But I am convinced it is time well spent. It may be one of the few chances you have to help an adult couple, who are well disposed, understand how marriage is holy. A parish normally has many married couples; yet often they have little chance to reflect on this aspect of their marriage. A parish can be really alive only if its adult members have a mature Christianity. Marriage is one of the most important religious experiences most lay people have. Living their married Christian life is their responsibility in the Church. The wedding ceremony with which they start it is also their responsibility. Our temptation can be to make too many of their decisions for them – sometimes even at their request!

'The couple's first choice may not be their last', as the Pastoral Notes (*The Celebration of Marriage*, page 6) says. 'Shy couples tend to opt at first for the "easier" formulary which demands the simple answer "I do". They should be invited to look more closely at the strength and warmth of the longer formularies, before making a final decision. The couple should be shown the "prayer of the newly-married couple" and asked if they would prefer to make up their own.'

If you have direct pastoral responsibility for their preparation, some or all of this area could perhaps be included at that stage; if not, you could check with them what was covered. It may not have been covered at all.

As a group of Christians celebrate the liturgy, some agreed form is needed. But it's never an 'instant liturgy' – a fixed form to which you just add people, and there you have the finished item. Rather, it is a very special type of event. This is particularly obvious in a wedding, where the worship is occasioned by an act of two specific individuals. What they do really is an act of worship. The ceremony should show that as clearly as possible. Your liturgical role in the celebration should be seen in the celebration; you are a witness representing the local Christian community and the whole Church. The celebration should also make very clear that the ministers of the sacrament of marriage are the couple themselves. This can be underlined, for example, not just by what they say, but also by the place they occupy in the assembled community as they minister the sacrament to one another. Even where they stand can give witness of this to the congregation.

Much modern life seems to be controlled by impersonal factors. If everything about marriage can be seen to be explicitly personal and holy, it will be a step towards bringing out the personal and holy in wider social relationships.

PART I

INTRODUCING CHRISTIAN MARRIAGE

A VERY PARTICULAR WEDDING

Think of a crowd – a very big crowd. Everyone going their own way. Nothing special about any of them. All may look more or less the same. All lead more or less the same kind of life, as far as we can see. Imagine yourself as one of them: as one of the crowd.

Except that you're not just one of the crowd. Out of all those people, you are the one that someone has chosen to love and marry. To that person, you are someone special – just because you're you. There has never been a couple quite like the two of you before.

You can see one another, know one another, love one another, touch one another. You're alive to each other. No one else is alive in quite the same way as each of you is alive. And nobody else can live your life for you.

You live your own life, each of you. There's an awful lot you can't do anything about in the world. You can't even change the way you were brought up. But you can live your own life – and nobody else can do it for you. Only you can make up your own mind.

You've decided to get married. That's another thing nobody else can do for you – you've got to do it yourself. And you've met someone who has chosen you. You mean a lot to one another. You love one another. You want a wedding. You don't go along to a supermarket and buy one, wrapped up and labelled and priced. A wedding is not something you get – not even from a priest. It's something you do. It's something most engaged couples have never done before.

The world we live in is full of marketing, looking for consumers. You may be dealing with many different commercial businesses which can help you in making your arrangements. It may even appear that Christian marriage is one of the consumer choices you can select, and which your Church is there to provide. To put it so starkly can appear strange; it's good to be aware of it, so you can guard against letting this creep into your approach to celebrating your wedding.

This book is not going to tell you exactly what to do. I could have picked out parts for everyone to say and do – that would have been much easier and very much shorter to write. But there would have been something missing – your choice. If you choose the parts yourselves, you can be sure your hearts are in them. I'm sure you could put your heart and soul into a fixed ceremony, just as much as you could into a marriage that was arranged completely by other people, even down to whom you would marry. A great number of people have in fact done that. But you can put yourself more easily into something you choose yourself.

You've decided for yourselves that you want to get married. This book is to help you make it your special wedding. You can choose a lot. Don't just say to the priest, 'Whatever you say, Father.' It's not his wedding – it's yours. A lot of things before and after the ceremony need to be arranged as well. Wouldn't it be strange to go to a lot of trouble over other things and none at all about what will happen at the wedding itself? The priest can help you, of course. But you can do your own planning. You'll find it worth while. Whatever thoughts and ideas you have for the future, perhaps you can put some of them into the way you plan your wedding.

It's not the priest's wedding, it's yours.

It's good to feel successful. We like to feel we're getting somewhere, doing something worthwhile. When you're married, it won't be just two people who happen to be living together. There'll be something entirely new. That's something very well worth while. Getting married is one of the most creative things you'll ever do. You'll be beginning a new kind of life, a new way of thinking and loving and living, a new life that will go on growing – a life not in the clouds, but down to earth.

Love is not in the clouds. You know you love one another because of particular things you do and say at particular times in particular places. And getting married is not in the clouds either. Getting married is a very particular way of living in love – living as husband and wife. 'You can't keep sex in the clouds; it is obviously in bed. What is more, it is in pillow-cases which were Aunt Emily's wedding present.' That's how Rosemary Haughton, a mother of nine children, puts it.

Everything important you do is particular. Be particular about your wedding too.

A suggestion: Perhaps you would like to take a section or two of this part of the book, 'Introducing Christian Marriage', each week or every few days, for each of you to read, and then sit down together (over light refreshments?) and talk about what, if anything, you make of it. Does that sound like 'homework'? It is homework – not work somebody gives you to do at home, but work towards the building of your home together.

A CHANGE OF LIFE

When you marry, you're not just deciding to live together and go on as you were; you're choosing a whole new lifestyle.

You'll find that your marriage is different – everybody's is. Anything important deserves to be talked about. Your marriage is one of the most important things in your lives. Up to now, the main link has been with whatever family or group you've grown up with. Now each of you is going to change that; your most important link in future will not be with the people you grew up with, but with the person you marry – the person you want to share your life and live with for maybe the next fifty years. Everything important changes you – it changes your life.

Religion is many things. The various religions, in many ways, are ways of making some sense of life – what it means to be alive, to be human, in this world, in the many stages we grow through in life.

Many people say there's no meaning to life. Many give answers different from yours. Being a Christian means that you find that Jesus Christ helps you to understand your life. Having your wedding in a church is your way of saying what this part of your life means to you as a Christian. As you work through the possibilities for your own wedding, keep asking yourselves: 'Which of these says best what getting married means to us?'

Getting married is the beginning of a big change in your way of life. Life is good and important – and holy. Being alive means so many things. It means being awake and doing things; and knowing what's going on around you and enjoying life; and growing; and loving. Loving and being loved means being more alive. Love is holy.

'Holy' and 'sacred' are two of the strongest words we have for saying that someone or something is important. A person, joking, may say something like, 'No – golf (or bingo, or something else) is not like a religion to me – it's much more important than that!' What is 'holy' or 'sacred' to you? What is there in your life that you would want to hold on to and protect, whatever the sacrifice? As you think of the person you commit your life to in love and marriage, can you apply the words 'holy' and 'sacred' here? Not something far away; not something that is not real to you; 'holy' means what is closer and dearer to you than you can find words for. This is true for when we say 'God is holy' too. Being alive is holy, in a very down-to-earth way. Married life is holy in a very down-to-earth way. Did you ever think of being married as a new way of holiness?

You can go on all your life learning more about one another, and there will still be something more to know: married life is a day-by-day process. This growing and deepening is what makes your life-long commitment to one another possible.

The Dublin-born writer, George Bernard Shaw, wrote: 'When two people are under the influence of the most violent, most insane, most delusive, and most transient of passions, they are required to swear that they will remain in that excited, abnormal, and exhausting state continuously until death do them part'.

But he was wrong. If he were right, marriage would be madness. What he describes can be part of our lives, and can be exciting. It is valuable and helpful to recognise the truth of what our feelings are at particular times. But your commitment in marriage is governed, not by feelings (which can change with the weather and with many other things), but by your decision that you will love the one you marry for better, for worse, for richer, for poorer, in sickness and in health, all your lives. This is something far more solid and dependable. If it is also inspired by the kind of love we see in Jesus Christ, you have an extra source of strength.

In two of the readings from letters of St Paul (Romans 12 on page 134 and Colossians on page 144), he talks about 'holy people', saints. Not people who have 'gone to their reward', but people like yourselves; people who may not always live like saints, but who want to live a true and full life, as Jesus did in living and in laying down his life; and married people who want to live that love together.

Remember 'Holy Days'? Your wedding day will be a Holy Day.

HOW DEEP IS YOUR LOVE?

You may have seen cartoons in newspapers, and greeting cards on sale, trying to say that 'Love is…' this or that. Some can be true and inspiring; some may be superficial; some may be false; some may even be quite offensive! Whatever we may say, genuine love is beyond what words can say. What I say in this section is simply my attempt to put into words that love, as Christian tradition understands it, goes deeper and higher and wider than we ever suspect. This goes for married love as well. I hope this will make some sense to you now, and even more in the future.

Love is like peace. Peace is not so much a destination I long to arrive at, nor the way I feel inside; it's much more the way I live today, the way I travel the road of life today. Love, too, is a way of life – the way I live each day; a way of thinking and acting and speaking. It can be as comfortable as a pair of old shoes, or as fresh as a new coat. It has moments when you can go about your activities, so absorbed that you're not consciously aware of the other person; and it has moments when you're so close that you're hardly two people, but one. Love is something bigger than you or me, or all of us together. (The reading from chapter 4 of the first letter of St John on page 149 actually says that God is love!) When you're married, your love will show itself in the way it takes you over as you make love, and in the way it guides the ordinary, everyday things you do.

In a way, your love hardly belongs to you – it's as if you belong to love. If the God we speak of is really the God of everything, then your love is an experience of God. God is love – strong and gentle and unconditional and close and holy. It's hard to believe that someone loves you if he or she does not show it. You can't love in theory without putting it into practice. God shows you love by creating the world, and the people in it; and by creating you. You experience God's love for you in the way you love one another as husband and wife. And in giving yourselves to one another in love, in the many different ways you do this, it's not just your own love you give; you also give, and receive, God's love from one another. Could you think of your love as a reflection of God's love? Even more than a reflection – could you think of your love as the 'embodiment' of God's love – God's love made real in you? This is part of what we mean when we say that marriage is a 'sacrament' of God's love.

Your marriage is deeper than just the two of you loving one another and deciding to make the rest of your lives together. It will be one of your most important ways of coming close to God. It begins on your wedding day, and lasts all your life. Clearly, you won't be always thinking about God, any more than you will be thinking of one another every moment of every day; but that does not mean that you don't love one another, any more than it would mean that God has vanished from your life. The God that Jesus lets us know is the God always with you, through the bright days and through the dark days. A God who is there, not to write down every mistake to charge you with, but the God of intimacy and tenderness and compassion and love. The God of your love for one another. The God of your ordinary everyday love, and the God of the closest and most intimate times of your love.

Think about your love for a minute: your love for one another now, and on your wedding day; your love a month later, a year later, then, twenty, fifty years later. How you will keep on showing your love. How close and how deep it is now and how close and deep it will be. That's how God loves you, too. That's what the sacrament of marriage means: your love gives an idea of what God's love is like. It's some of God's love in action.

Have you something concrete to aim at? How about something like this: to be able to say each wedding anniversary, *'This last year has been the best year of all so far in our love!'*

WHY COMPLICATE IT WITH RELIGION?

Sometimes it seems that religion makes things more complicated and difficult than they really are; whereas exactly the opposite should be the case! So I hope these few pages will make some sense.

It's not so much 'bringing religion into it', as seeing where human life and sexuality and marriage are already involved with our relationship with God. If you look at the first of the scripture readings from the book of Genesis (you'll find it on page 111), there's a simple story with a valuable insight: the sexual relationship between a man and a woman is not something evil or shameful, made grudgingly permissible by marriage; nor is it a god to control our whole lives. Rather, it is one of God's greatest gifts to us: 'God saw that it was very good!'

What do we normally mean by 'gift'? When you give someone a birthday present, it's as if you were saying something like 'I'm glad you were born, and that you're here now!' It's something more than just a 'thing' that we get or give. It's a means of communication – a means by which the giver says something, and the receiver accepts the message as well as the gift. It's an encounter between persons.

If we talk about sexuality and marriage as a gift, what could that mean? Your marriage involves many things. Deep down, as you meet one another, it is an encounter with God.

Hard to believe? That God, who is so 'super-spiritual', can touch you in something as earthly as your marriage? This is one of the wonderful insights that the coming of Jesus gives us. Jesus is our 'God with us'. Jesus was born in a place as real as the place you were born in. (Read about it in chapter 2 of St Luke's Gospel.) A birth is a very flesh-and-blood experience. Jesus needed the kind of looking after that any baby needs – feeding, and cuddling, and cleaning. And yet we say that in Jesus, we meet God!

Yes, it is hard to believe – just as hard to believe that you can encounter the presence of God in your marriage. But if you let Jesus into your lives, you can discover for yourselves the truth of it. And not just in the 'loving' times. The end of the life of Jesus was not a warm, comforting, 'spiritual' experience: it, too, was a very flesh-and-blood experience. And yet we say that here, too, we are touched by the love of God in Jesus Christ. If you put a reminder of Jesus in your home as a married couple, it can help you keep something of all this in mind.

We are human beings, flesh and blood. It is in and through our human lives that we meet God; are touched by God. Jesus spoke about his Father; and about the Father's love for him and for us; and about our loving one another. Jesus also promised to be with us all days, until the end of time. But then Jesus went away. Does this mean we've just got to accept this, with no experience of Jesus being with us? The first followers of Jesus faced this too. And they made a remarkable discovery. When we sincerely follow Jesus, and love one another as followers of Jesus, we discover that something else happens too. We find that love is rather bigger than we thought (and often not as easy either!), but we begin to recognise that, in some extraordinary way, Jesus is with us. It is true what Jesus said: 'Wherever two or three come together in my name, I am there among them' (St Matthew's Gospel, chapter 18, verse 20).

Can I prove it? No. Can you prove that you love someone? You may do all the things that normally seem to indicate love, but love is something beyond these; it's sad that we can use these signs of love when love is not genuinely there, for our own selfish reasons or from thoughtlessness. Knowing that someone loves you is something almost beyond all proof. And knowing that the love of God is very much there in our love is something we just have to experience for ourselves. Like riding a bike, or swimming, or knowing personally what living a marriage is, it's something nobody else can do for you. You have to experience it for yourself.

WHERE DOES 'SACRAMENT' COME IN?

As the years and centuries went by, there were further developments: Christians began to realise more clearly that this experience of the touch of God who is love is realised in a special way in some particular human experiences – ways we now call *Sacraments*. Just as you can express and give love in a sign that we call a handshake or a kiss, the realisation grew that in marriage we have a special sign of God's love for his people.

You could look at it something like this. Two people who marry give an unconditional promise to love one another for better, for worse, for richer, for poorer, in sickness and in health, all the days of their lives. This is a sign for each of them that that's the kind of love that God has for them too: an unconditional, eternal love. The commitment *'to love you for better, for worse, for richer, for poorer, in sickness and in health, all the days of our life'* is a sign that God promises to be faithful to us no matter how unfaithful we may be. A wedding service in an old York Manual which may go back to the fourteenth century adds 'for fayrere for fowlere' – that is, 'whether you're more beautiful or more ugly'!

Not only that, but in showing that love to one another, each partner gives the other not just his or her own love, but is actually a channel of God's love for the other person. And looking beyond the couple themselves, their faithful love for one another, is a sign to their local community and to the world that this kind of love really is possible; so that we can look at the couple who are a living example of it and say *'There must be something more to this: there's something divine about it: God has a hand in this!'* Every way a wife and husband have of loving one another, from the simplest expression of friendship, to washing socks or digging a garden, to the most intimate act of love – all these can actually bring the couple both closer to one another *and closer to God at the same time.* You might say that they make saints of one another by loving one another! Isn't that what bringing someone closer to God means? Before marriage, you might say, each makes his or her own way to God within the Christian community. Now, as a married couple, they are together a living sacrament in the Christian community: a living sign and instrument of God's love for one another and for the world.

That's something of what it means to say that *'marriage is a sacrament'*. Not just that there's a blessing for you on the day of your wedding; not just that God wants you to live according to his rules in your marriage. The gift is that you are enabled to be an extraordinary gift of divine love to one another and to the world.

Since so much of this may seem extraordinary, I may as well add one final extraordinary thought. You may remember learning in school that marriage is a sacrament (although you probably did not hear about the strange things on the last few pages!). So, if marriage is a sacrament – well, marriage doesn't just happen in a church building, even if, for Christians, it normally starts there. Marriage is mostly outside the church building. Just as a song can't exist without a singer (a song on paper is not fully a song until it is sung), in the same way, you can't have marriage without the people. So, if marriage is a sacrament, then you, the man and woman who are living your marriage, are a sacrament. A living sacrament. Everywhere, every moment. You are a living sign and channel of God's love for one another and for the world.

Say this together, looking at one another: 'We are a living sacrament!' And if you feel like smiling, or falling around the place laughing, so much the better. Because it is crazy. And wonderful. And true.

BUT NORMAL PEOPLE DON'T FIND THAT!

Dr Patricia Marshall wrote:

> *It is precisely through their love for each other that husbands and wives make Christ present to each other. Married people may have read this with some disbelief. It is hard to believe it. When a woman sees her husband coming home tired and bad tempered after work (or after a depressing day with no work); when he sees his wife chasing the children to bed with nothing ready for him to eat, then I don't think the first thought that strikes most of us is 'Ah, yes, here we are making Christ present to each other.'*
>
> *We're slow enough to see this even in happier moments. It all seems so ordinary, so human. But it is just this ordinary human relationship of marriage which has the extraordinary possibility of showing us Christ – or rather letting Christ show himself to us. How? By showing us, by teaching us, what love is. And we do need to learn.*
>
> (*Christian Encounter:* Redemptorist Publications,
> Alton, Hants, 5 August 1973.)

So there's a problem about all this; if what I say is true, why don't married couples normally seem to know it or be aware of it at all? Some couples do have an awareness of it – I have certainly met some who have told me so. But it's not spoken of very often – it's such a personal thing.

There's another factor involved too. Long before you actually knew the meaning of 'love', there was love in your live. We normally experience love from a very early age – from parents, family etc. – long before we learn to recognise it as love. But it is not any less truly love, even if we don't recognise it. In fact, it can very often take an adult many years to begin to appreciate the love his or her parents gave; it can take a lifetime for a husband or wife to appreciate the love his or her partner gave. Some may never realise it at all. We can receive the love God gives us in just as real a way as we can accept the love of our parents and families, even if we don't realise at the time that is happening. Perhaps only by thinking back on it later, and by talking about our experience with others, or when we feel we have lost the one who loves us, do we come to realise something of the love we receive, either from one another or from God. If we could become better at sharing this sort of experience with one another, and overcome our shyness about it, our lives could be greatly enriched. This then could help us be more aware of what is happening in our experience of loving and being loved. To say 'marriage is a sacrament' could go further than being a piece of Religious Knowledge, and become something we know from experience. It could be a source of strength and joy, not a puzzle or a complication.

COULD WE WORK ON IT?

Before a couple marry it would be good if they could talk together about who God is for them; and to share it also as they grow and develop through the years that follow. Many couples planning to marry will have shared with each other about nearly everything else, even the most personal things, but perhaps not about what part religion plays in their life. How you pray is very personal. That's good. But that doesn't mean you have to keep it all to yourself. Wouldn't it be strange if this were the one and only part of you that you never got to share with one another? How much do you know about this side of each other? What do you think you know about your partner's experience in these matters? Maybe you could tell each other. Here is a suggestion to help you start; you may have other ideas of your own.

Take half an hour, or an hour, or as long as you want. Each of you takes a blank sheet of paper, and draws a line down the centre from top to bottom. Write the first of the following questions right across the top, and on the left of the line, write how you think your partner would answer it; on the right side of the line, write how you answer it for yourself. Then write the second question across below that, and answer both sides.

The questions are just to help you focus on what your own experience of faith and religion and God may have been. If any question does not seem to apply to you, or doesn't make sense to you, just skip over it. 'Don't know' is an okay answer! If reading or writing is a problem for either of you, perhaps you can find another way to approach this.

Don't be afraid to make mistakes: there are no bad marks for not doing well. Don't worry about the spelling of the words. What is important is that they are the truth about what you know. Your first answer may not be your last one. Some memories can be buried very deep. It may be a voyage of discovery, both into your own life and into the life of the one you plan to marry.

When you're both finished, exchange the pages with some simple sign of affection. Then read what the other has written. Read it with respect and reverence: what's written can be very personal and private. Don't read it to disagree or criticise, but to understand. Be prepared perhaps to be surprised.

When you're both ready, talk about what you find there. Be honest with one another. The purpose is not to criticise or to correct, but to understand and to accept and to love. See have you learned anything about one another.

Put a marker in this page, and take as much time out for this as you want!

1. How often do I think about God?
2. Was there ever a time in my life when I felt the nearness of God?
   Was there ever a time in my life when I felt really far from God?
3. When I think about Jesus Christ, how do I feel – warm? cold? nothing?
4. Does Jesus Christ influence my life? If so, how?
5. Do I pray every day? about once a week? occasionally? rarely?
6. How do I pray when I'm alone? Kneeling, or sitting, or standing, or lying in bed? Eyes open or closed? Before a statue or picture or crucifix, or wherever? At home, in a church, out in the open?
7. Do I pray in my own words, or in words I learned by heart, or from a book or leaflet?
   Do I pray sometimes without words?
8. Do I have a favourite prayer? a favourite piece from the Bible?
9. To whom do I pray? God the Father? Jesus Christ? The Holy Spirit? Mary? A favourite saint?
10. Did my family ever pray together when I was growing up? If so, how? How did I find it?
11. When we are together, do I ever have a sense of God's love for us?
12. Any other question or comment in this area that strikes me?

When you have shared these things with one another, you might like to talk further about some more aspects of your life together, arising from your answers. Again, some of these may not apply to everyone.

Have we gone to Mass together?
Have we ever prayed together, apart from at Mass?
Could we pray when we're alone together, either in silence or aloud?
Could we pray a prayer that we are both familiar with?
Could either of us pray aloud with the other, in our own words?
What about when we are married, what will we do?
If and when, please God, we have children, what will we do?
Could we tell one another about our difficulties in faith as well as our strengths?
If your faith is strong, how will that affect me?
If your faith is weak, how will that affect me?
How can my relationship with God affect you?
How can your relationship with God affect me?

If you can get around to sharing these things with one another, and to praying with one another, you may find that it can give your relationship an entirely new dimension that you may not have suspected. You may find, too, that at times when your relationship with one another is at its best, your relationship with God will also be at its best.

DOES THE CHURCH NEED TO BE INVOLVED WITH OUR MARRIAGE?

This question may well be the strangest one to get your teeth into, because many people's experience of being the Church is so far from the 'vision' of what the Church is called to be. But this may be the best time in your life to tackle it because right at this time you yourselves are aiming for what a song calls 'The Impossible Dream'. Your aiming at that 'dream', and your working at it together, can very well help to bring us closer at the same time to the 'vision' of what we, the Church, are called to be: people united in a love that is eternal.

The Church is involved for exactly the same reason that you may want your families and friends to be involved. The Church is (or is meant to be!) a community of people, united in our faith, in helping one another to follow Jesus Christ, and in wanting to bring his message and life to the world. If your intention is to have a church wedding, it must mean in some way, even if for some not too strongly, that you are part of the life of that community of the Church, and that community is part of your life.

After all, if you are not in any way a part of the community of the Church, why would you want a church wedding at all? Just because it's a location you like, or because it's the tradition in your family – are these good reasons for wanting a church wedding? On the other hand, if you have not been a part of the community of the Church in any real way in recent years, now would be a good time to talk together about how you can begin to find your way back. Your church wedding, and your marriage afterwards, would then mean so much more than just renting the building for a day, and hiring a priest for the job.

Usually you tell your family and friends about your wedding, and, where possible, invite them to the wedding. You will need at least two people there as witnesses of what you're doing, as well as the minister who 'assists'. Sadly, it may not often be as obvious how the 'Church' – that is, the community of Christians – is involved, except as the 'official' body you go to to get married. This may be due to how anonymous and distant our experience of our Church and our parish can be – we who are the Church have a lot of work to do in this sphere. Yet it is still true that every real follower of Jesus Christ is a member of the one Body, all a part of one another. On page 138 you'll see a reading from chapter 13 of St Paul's first letter to the Corinthians: a familiar one about the gift of love. Get a copy of the Bible or the New Testament (the Christian writings in our Bible), and read the chapter before that: chapter 12 – different gifts as members of the body, all sharing the one Spirit. One writer describes Christian marriage like this:

> *It is a call, a vocation from God through the Church that asks the couple, 'Will you please spend your love for each other for us? Will you allow us to look at you as a sign of how we are to love one another in the Church? When we gather with you, will you touch us by your tenderness and desire for each other? Will you be responsible to us in how you live your life together? Will you allow us to continue to call you to live your life of unity more totally and completely as time goes by? ...even at those times when you do not feel like forgiving and healing one another?' ...As in Ordination, the primary focus of matrimony as a sacrament is the Church, while the central focus in non-sacramental marriage is on the couple and their family. Matrimony as a sacrament does not ignore the focus of simple marriage, it includes and transcends it for the well-being of the Church.* (Thomas L. Vandenberg: *A Sign for Our Time – The Sacrament of Matrimony:* Veritas Parish and Family Resources, Dublin, 1982)

The Church is involved because it was through the Church that you received life as a Christian. Not the Church as a building you meet in; not the Church as it can appear to be, just the full-time officials; but the Church as the Body of people who find that, as followers of Jesus, they have a tremendous bond of unity, and who value each and every member of the Body.

And now that you are planning to live a Christian marriage together, this is a cause of great joy for the members of the Body. Living your Christian marriage will actually be a proclaiming of the Gospel, the Good News of God who is Love – and has the possibility of touching more people than many a sermon in church on Sunday! The Church stands with you as you make your commitment and as you accept this gift from God, and its presence there is a promise of solidarity with you over all the years of your marriage. In marrying in the Church, you ask the Church to support you in your times of joy and your times of difficulty and sorrow – that is a gift from the rest of the Church to you.

Your gift to the Church as a couple will be that you teach us how to grow in our loving. When you 'make love', that is exactly what you will do, for yourselves, and the Church, and the world. Love is not like a store of credit that we use up some of each time we 'make love', until finally some day it may just run out; rather, each time you or I act in love, we make love grow greater.

> *This doesn't only happen through sexual intercourse, but through all the experiences of love that a couple share. Not only through the tender affectionate experiences, not only the sacrifices they make, but also through the mistakes, inadequacies and rows. Married quarrels are among the bitterest there are. Only people who know each other well know exactly where to put the knife to hurt most. And this can be destructive. But it doesn't need to be if only we remain willing to learn. Willing to learn about ourselves and our own failures, willing to learn about our partners and to accept their shortcomings, willing in a word to learn about love.* (Dr Patricia Marshall)

The Church *needs* to learn from you, as well as you from the Church.

That isn't the kind of Church you know! I'm sure a great many Christians would say the same. We who are the Church fail to live up to the reality of what we are. You, too, if you are human, will have your failures as you find that loving is not always as easy a way of life as we sometimes expect. We are called to so much more than we are at present. We need to be reminded and encouraged again and again. Your married life could be an inspiration: the dedication and sacrifice and forgiveness you gladly put into your love for one another is a challenge to the Church. With all the faults and failings a Christian marriage or family may have, it is what is sometimes called 'the Church of the home', the 'domestic Church'. The personal touch a home can have is a challenge to the rest of the Church to imitate that. Just imagine if we did just that!

BUT THE CHURCH IS SO AGAINST EVERYTHING!

Why is it that so often Church teaching about marriage and sexuality seems to come across as 'Thou shalt not!'? And the way it has been communicated at times has not always been the happiest. It can seem so different to what Jesus says: *'I have come so that they may have life – life in all its fullness'* (St John's Gospel, chapter 10, verse 10). That is the purpose of all his teaching, and of the teaching of the Church.

If you're looking after a small child in a room with a fire, and you see the child approaching the fire, you might say: 'Don't go near that fire!' and you could very well have to repeat it. Why? Perhaps because you're afraid you'll be blamed if anything happens to the child; but if you love the child, it will much more likely be because you don't want the child to be hurt. Certainly not because you don't want the child to have fun, or to learn something new; nor just because you'll be offended at the child doing something you said not to do!

To take some examples: when the commandments or the teaching of the Church tell us 'Thou shalt not commit adultery', it's for the same reason: that God, in his love for us, doesn't want us to come to harm, but wants us to be fully alive, with all possible joy in living and loving. But like with the child, we may not always appreciate it like that! In the same way, for example, the teaching about not having sexual intercourse with a person you're not at the time married to is not intended to deprive you, but precisely to enrich your life.

This is an area where many people find a considerable problem. The very idea of not having sex except within marriage seems totally unrealistic and outrageous. Any suggestion that it is not wise to live together as a husband and wife for some months or perhaps years before getting married, seems very old-fashioned, at the very least.

Having sexual intercourse is portrayed often as simply a normal recreation without much deeper meaning than going to a film or for a drink together. It is taken as meaning no more than a particularly warm handshake; just more enjoyable. Even the idea of 'Never have sex on a first date' is irrelevant where the purpose of going out for the night is to 'score' or 'get laid' (or whatever words are used at the particular place and time), and it may not even matter who the other person is: may not even be known. If, for one person involved, 'Last night didn't really mean anything', while for the other person it seemed that it did mean something significant – well, that's just one hurt or disappointment you've just got to learn to get over. Many of you may have had the experience of being shattered in a sexual relationship. There can be a lot of pressure on people to go along with what 'everybody is doing'. There can be pressure from within where two people know they are ready to make a lasting commitment, but 'we can't afford to have a wedding yet' – so why not live together until we can afford the big day?

This book is not the place to discuss all this in depth. There are many serious implications for how men and women relate, and especially for the long-term relationship of marriage. There are also many serious implications for physical health. What I do want to present here is an understanding that each and every person, man and woman and child, is immensely precious and valuable, and, as a child of God, never to be used by another just as a means of pleasure, but to be loved and cherished. Sex does in fact have a deeply inter-personal value – it is not just contact of body-parts. I do want to present an understanding of marriage, and of our sexuality, as among the greatest and most enriching experiences in human life, and in the life of Christians.

Each person or couple reading this will have their own situation and experience. Please read what follows, and discuss it together. Talk about what you find good in what you read and understand. Talk as well about what you're inclined to reject. If there are implications for your life as you prepare for marriage, you can work things out together with faith and trust in your love of one another. If you have got this far, it probably means that your religious faith is valuable in your life; so it would be good to pray, separately or together or both, to ask God to let the Spirit of love guide you as to what is best in your situation.

In our Christian tradition (which much of the world would not accept), the fullest expression of love in intercourse is a way of saying 'We are fully committed to one another, and we intend to be always faithful to one another in love, just as God is always faithful to us'. To use the means of expressing that, when it is not true that the partners are fully committed to one another, is false, and harmful to both partners – whether they realise it or not. If there is falsity involved, it is not 'true love'; although it looks exactly the same as 'making love', rather it is 'making sex'. Even if the two partners genuinely love one another, the fact is that there is something false in the expression of their love.

When two people love each other very much, each will genuinely find happiness in doing whatever is really good for the other. In 'the heat of the moment' it can be difficult to be aware that what you feel you really want at that moment may not be what is really true love, even if you have talked it over together fully many times. It is something that has to be learned. And if there are failures to be 'true lovers' – remember that for human beings, forgiveness is as much a part of God's love for us as it must be of our love for one another.

The same loving purpose is behind all the other teachings and commandments. You might like to talk with one another about other aspects of what our Christian tradition says in relation to our sexuality, both for single people and married people, and see if you can make sense of it in your own situation.

WHAT'S LOVE GOT TO DO WITH IT?

There's a song which asks: *'What can I do to make you love me?'* Sometimes what we think is love gets very mixed up with other motives. Love is not something we can make a person give. If someone says, as the words of another song go: *'She's so beautiful, I know I've got to have her!'* – is that love? It may sound very flattering, but it also sounds more like lust, or greed, or selfishness – it certainly is not focused on what will bring joy and life to the other.

True love is always a gift given freely. Fr Tony de Mello tells a story:

> *Once upon a time long ago and far away, there was a man who wanted very much for a woman to notice him, to fall in love with him. He went to a wizard, who gave him a love potion to do what he wanted. He slipped the potion in her glass, and she looked at him and fell in love with him. They had a wonderful wedding with all their friends and relations.*
>
> *A month later the man woke up one day and realised he was not at all happy. He had everything he had wished for, and still there was something wrong. He went back to the wizard to make his complaint. The wizard listened, and then he answered: 'I gave you what you asked for. But what you say now tells me that that was not what you wanted. Now you don't know whether she would have come to love you for who you are, if you had not given her the love potion'.*

We can be side-tracked from the way of love. It's good to be aware of this, so we can keep our eyes open! We love to be around the people we love. But if another person says to you: '*I need you – I can't live without you!*' – whose happiness does this focus on? Does it set you free, or possess you?

Sexual love clearly has an important place in marriage. But it is not what marriage is all about. Sexual love, expressed too strongly and too early in a relationship, may prevent the relationship maturing. It is a mistake to expect sex alone to sustain a relationship indefinitely. Even though it is sometimes called a 'relationship', there may in fact be no relationship of two people whatsoever.

It takes time to grow and mature in love. We need to give it time; we need to make the time, even when it seems we are 'wasting time' when we could be 'doing' so much else. From the first meeting, to the growing interest in the other person, to the first steps in a commitment; and so it goes, until we meet a time when, perhaps all of a sudden, we realise, 'It's not as easy to love as I used to think!' We discover that love is not about 'I've got to do first what makes me happy – right?' Rather, the amazing promise the bride and groom make at the wedding says:

I take you as my husband/wife
for better, for worse, for richer, for poorer,
in sickness and in health, all the days of our life.

Loving, and marriage, do not fulfil all of a person's wants and needs for the rest of their life. In true love, and in marriage, we learn that we do not have the power to be everything to the one we love. In times of trouble or sickness or bereavement, we may feel helpless even to bring comfort. This very powerlessness is made all the more acute by the depth of our love. This can be a sign that love is finding its growing pains; its steps towards maturity.

A German writer, Dietrich Bonhoeffer, wrote:

Nothing can fill the gap when we are away from those we love,
and it would be wrong to try to find anything.
We must simply hold out and win through ...
leaving the gap unfilled preserves the bond between us.
It is nonsense to say 'God fills the gap':
he does not fill it, but keeps it empty
so that our communion with one another
may be kept alive, even at the cost of pain.
The dearer and richer our memories, the more difficult the separation.
But gratitude converts the pangs of memory into a tranquil joy.

Here, we who are followers of Jesus Christ can remember that the way of love is also the way of the cross. Jesus said that there is no greater love, than to lay down your life for your friend, the one you love. Not that we foolishly look for 'the cross'; nor that we carry the cross resentfully, or angrily, but in love. Remember how you can be willing to do extraordinary things, make great sacrifices, for the one you love, and do it willingly and freely and joyfully. The early

Christians saw that there is a close connection between how Jesus laid down his life freely in love for his people (the 'Church'), and how a husband and wife lay down their lives freely in love for one another. This is the 'mystery' St Paul mentions in his letter to the Ephesians (reading on page 141).

We can look, as Jesus did on the cross, into the darkness; we may even feel totally abandoned; and still, even here, we hold on to our faith in the one or ones we love. We may not see how, but, with Jesus, we live by the knowledge that no cross can overcome the God of love, the love God gives us for one another. We live Good Friday and Easter Sunday. As Jesus said to Peter, speaking of the Church, the community of his followers who would be known by their love: 'The gates of hell can never overpower it'. As the letter of St Paul to the Corinthians on page 138 says:

> *Love is always patient and kind; love is never jealous;*
> *love is not boastful or conceited, it is never rude and never seeks its own advantage; it does not take offence or store up grievances.*
> *Love does not rejoice at wrongdoing, but finds its joy in the truth.*
> *It is always ready to make allowances, to trust, to hope and to endure whatever comes. Love never comes to an end.*

A WEDDING SAYS WHAT?

Of course, we all know what a wedding is. We know what walking is, what a football match is, what love is. But it can be hard to put it into words. You may like to try to put into words your understanding of the meaning of your wedding. You might describe what could be seen of your wedding on television – that is, what can be seen on the outside. But try as well to say what the *real* event will be: what happens between the bride and groom in their hearts; what happens between you not just as a man and woman, but also as people who follow the way of Jesus.

I'd like to offer some suggestions to get you chewing! See whether these ring a wedding bell with you; change them as much as you want till you get nearer to what *you* would say.

> Your wedding is when you say in public:
> *'We belong to each other in love for the rest of our lives from this moment on, and we want you all to recognise it!'*
>
> Before your witnesses and your world, you say:
> *'The two of us here are going to live in a way that will show how much we love each other. We believe in living for each other – this will make us even more alive. Whatever kind of people we are now, and whatever we may be like in the future, we each promise to love the other unconditionally for the rest of our lives. Whatever hurts we may have, our love will be still stronger. We believe God is inspiring our love. Our love will tell you something of how much God loves. We need your help and your love to support us in this dream. We want you to know about our dream, and to share in it. We want you to take heart from us. We believe that life and love will never die.'*

If each of you is a person who is clearly conscious that Jesus Christ is a vital inspiration in your life, perhaps the following 'Covenant' may provide you with ideas of how you see where you stand as you prepare to celebrate your wedding. If you belong to different Christian Churches, a Covenant something like this may provide a sound basis of how your faith will be central in your marriage.

> *We freely make our decision to marry as followers of Jesus Christ.*
>
> *As we do so, we renew our faith in God, and in the living Jesus Christ, the son of God, risen from the dead.*
>
> *Jesus, in his life, death and resurrection, is the inspiration and guide light of our lives, the one who frees us from the power of sin and evil, and who gives us a new way to live, both as individuals, and as a married couple.*
>
> *In Jesus, and in the love of Jesus for his Body, the Church, God has*

given us the free gift of his covenant of everlasting love, by the Holy Spirit whom we have received.

In giving ourselves to one another as husband and wife, we two become one flesh whom God joins together as a loving sign of his covenant.

We intend, by God's grace, to love each other truly, for better, for worse, for richer, for poorer, in sickness and in health, so long as we both shall live.

We will, each of us, by God's grace, do everything possible to grow together as husband and wife in the unity of faith, and to avoid all danger of falling away from our faith and from each other, and to respond to the call to be active Church members.

Whenever difficulties between us threaten to become barriers separating us, we will look to Jesus, who is our peace, to overcome the barriers.

We will do everything possible, so far as in us lies, to bring up all the children of our marriage in the freedom of the children of God, and to share with them the riches of our Christian and Church traditions.

We will be always faithful to each other in love, learning to love each other as Jesus loves us – learning to be always patient and kind, ever learning not to be jealous, or rude, or selfish; to delight not in each other's failings, but rather in the truth of the gift each of us is to the other; to be ready always to excuse, to trust, to hope, and to endure whatever comes, knowing that love does not come to an end.

The language may be strange; but do these statements aim any higher than a couple themselves aim on their wedding day, even with all the other things on their minds? You know well that there are marriages that seem to work well, and marriages that run into difficulties. Love does not say there are no difficulties – love works on in spite of difficulties. Like Jesus Christ. You know his story. Now, that story is going to be your story as husband and wife. Your marriage is to show the power of love. It's so hard even to change the kind of words we speak. You can't depend on yourselves alone. But you can depend on

Jesus. He promised to stay with us all our days, to the very end of time. He knows what love is about. His love is unconditional. He never says 'That's the end – I've had enough'. A cross in your house is not just a normal, traditional decoration. It's a reminder of the extent of love.

Each of you may have a different way to say it, whether in a few words or in many. If you can find words of your own to say what your wedding will mean to your partner, or if you can find someone else's words that seem to say it for you, you may like to speak it out to one another. Or if you can, write it to one another in a letter of love; or have it set out in a form you could frame and hang on the wall of your home. And you may like to read it every year or every five years, and see how you would then express it more deeply.

As you plan your wedding, remember what you want to express and celebrate; so that people looking on from outside would get the meaning from what they see and hear.

INTERCHURCH AND INTERFAITH MARRIAGES

An 'interchurch' marriage is where bride and groom are members of two different Christian Churches. An 'interfaith' marriage is where one or other is not a baptised Christian. If you belong to different Christian Churches or communions, this is something you should take plenty of time to talk about together. The faith and the Church in which you were brought up can have a very deep effect on you and it's important to go on learning to understand each other. It can be helpful to get together with a minister from each Church to talk about it. Above all, remember that you already share something very important: your faith in Jesus Christ as your Lord.

If one of you is not a Christian, it is equally important to share what you believe in with each other. The experience of talking about faith in Jesus with someone who does not share it can teach a Christian a great deal; so can the experience of really listening to someone with quite a different background and outlook on life.

You are still as welcome in the Church for your wedding as any other couple. Coming to a Catholic church for your wedding may already be a sacrifice for the non-Catholic and his or her family. Arrangements for mixed marriages have changed a lot in recent years and may vary from place to place. Because of this, it is best to consult the priest in the parish where the wedding will take place. And you can still work on your wedding ceremony together, so that, as far as possible, it speaks for you both. Religion can still play an important part in your married life afterwards, where each of you respects deeply what the other regards as holy. In addition, the question of the upbringing of the children is one you will need to discuss deeply.

Where both of you are Christians, contact with other such couples can be good. The addresses at which to contact the Association of Interchurch Families are listed in Part V on page 242.

(The following is an extract from *Preparing for a Mixed Marriage*, published by Veritas for the Irish Episcopal Conference, 1983.)

If you are considering getting married to somebody who is not a Catholic, you may, in addition to all the usual hopes and problems of a person deciding to get married, have some questions about the implications of such a decision from a religious point of view.

As a general principle the Church discourages mixed marriages because they involve certain difficulties and tensions which we will look at in more detail later. This does not mean, however, that the Church will in any way seek to place obstacles in your path. You are not a 'general principle', but a couple who at this stage share a great deal at the level of affection and mutual understanding. The concern of the Church in your regard, therefore, will be to ensure that you appreciate as fully as possible the difficulties that you will face together so that you will be able to deal with them in a constructive and realistic way and so that they may not be a source of divisiveness in your marriage. In this way, you will be helped to live in your marriage the hopes as well as the difficulties of the path of Christian unity.

An outline of the difficulties which can arise may sound rather negative, but the positive values of your marriage will not emerge unless the difficulties are faced and realistically resolved.

If that is done, then there may indeed be very positive benefits to be found in mixed marriage. Each of you can learn to appreciate the values of another Christian tradition. You can contribute to the search for Christian unity not only by the tolerance and mutual respect you will foster in your own home but also by helping to increase understanding among your relatives and friends. This will demand from each of you a readiness to reflect on, and to learn more about, your own tradition in order to be able to share it. The Church is anxious to help you in any way possible to reach the necessary depth and maturity of knowledge which this will require.

It will also be important for you to express the hope for Christian unity in prayer together, as Pope John Paul II asked in his homily at York: 'Express that hope in prayer together, in the unity of love. Together invite the Holy Spirit of love into your hearts and into your homes. He will help you to grow in trust and understanding'.

Do we have to get married in the Catholic Church?

The general rule is that a Catholic must marry in the Catholic Church, or, to use the technical term, 'according to the canonical form'. Discussions between the Churches have not yet reached the point, except in relation to the Eastern Orthodox Church, at which the Catholic Church could give general recognition to mixed marriages which take place in another Church. This is mainly due to differences between the Churches with regard to the recognition of purely civil marriages and of divorce.

At the same time, in particular cases, where serious pastoral reasons may seem to warrant it, your local bishop will give sympathetic consideration to a request to allow the marriage to take place in the church, and according to the rites of, another denomination (cf. Pastoral Directory on Mixed Marriages *12). In this case, the Catholic Church fully recognises that ceremony as a sacramental marriage. If he is invited, and in accordance with the wishes of the minister of the other Church, a Catholic priest will attend and take part in the ceremony and say some additional prayers and blessings; as long as the marriage does not take place in conjunction with a celebration of the Lord's supper, he may read a lesson and preach. A Catholic priest may not, however, conduct the marriage ceremony according to the rites of another Church.*

While invitations to your wedding are obviously a matter for yourselves, the Catholic Church would wish that a minister of the other denomination should be present. If he attends, he will be given a place of honour in the sanctuary and he should be invited to say some words of greeting or exhortation and/or additional prayers and blessings. If there is no Nuptial Mass, he may read a lesson and preach. The wedding ceremony itself must, however, be conducted by a Catholic minister.

May we have Mass?

This is a matter for discussion between yourselves and the priest. Provided that your partner is baptised, the bishop will allow Mass, but you should first consider the options carefully. On the one hand, your partner and his or her family may not want to have Mass since they could not participate fully and would, perhaps, feel somewhat excluded from a ceremony in which they would wish to be fully involved. On the other hand, if your partner and the other family might interpret the omission of Nuptial Mass as expressing any lack of fraternal feeling towards them as fellow Christians, perhaps Mass should be celebrated.

PART II

PREPARING THE WAY

WHOM TO INVITE?

You may decide to have some, many, or no guests apart from the witnesses. You can plan this in many ways. Sometimes couples have a pre-wedding reception, or a reception some time afterwards. Sometimes couples send a piece of wedding cake to those who cannot make it to the wedding. Here I want to deal just with the day of the wedding.

So what about inviting people to your wedding ceremony? One way to approach it is this:

Make out a list of everyone you can possibly think of to invite. Then – invite them all! If your parishes have newsletters, put in an announcement some weeks beforehand – and invite every member of your parishes who can come!

Obviously I'm mad, you may be thinking.

But wait a minute. We're talking about your wedding. If you're using this book, it means you're planning to celebrate your wedding in a church. The only reason for not inviting everybody to be there is if the building simply will not hold them all. (The 'private' part of your wedding day is whatever reception you may have afterwards.) Imagine what it would be like to have a pretty full church for your wedding. Does it give you goose pimples? (Or goose bumps, if you're from North America.) Or would it make it more memorable?

But, but…

'But we couldn't possibly afford it all!'

Afford what? The parish doesn't charge you for every person who comes. It's your wedding celebration in the church. You don't have to invite everyone who comes to the church to come also for an expensive meal and dance afterwards. Perhaps you could; but aren't most people sensible enough to know that there are limits to that? Aren't they your family, your friends, your community, your parish? Will some of them be unhappy about it? Perhaps. But is it not strange to think that you can't invite people to your wedding celebration in the church – the very heart of your celebration – just because you can't provide a lavish meal for everyone afterwards? Or that you can only give them an 'Evening Invitation' after the meal, and not to where the heart of the action is?

'But nobody ever does that!'
How do you know? And even if it's true – why not be the first?

'They would all feel as if they had to give us a wedding gift.'
Maybe some would; but maybe you could trust their common sense.

'We would feel mean!'
Yes – you would like to be able to offer hospitality to everyone. Everyone knows it's not possible or reasonable. Perhaps you could be creative, and think up another way. Here are two alternative ways of going about it – and both of these have been done!

a. Is there a convenient local hall or place where you could invite everyone immediately after the wedding ceremony for simple, light refreshments (this could be stated on the invitation) – just tea / coffee / lemonade – and cut the wedding cake there and share it with everyone? Then, later, have a more private reception according to your situation. You yourselves might even appreciate a snack just after the wedding ceremony, if you will have to wait some hours for photographs, etc. before you get a meal.

b. Arrange a place where each person can come along for a meal, formal or informal, for which they pay themselves, or make a donation to cover the cost of it.

'But it's a working day – most people couldn't come!'
That's okay – you don't expect everyone you want to invite to be able to come. But it need not stop you letting them know you would

like them to be there to share your day, as you exchange your marriage vows.

'But we just want a small, quiet wedding!'
That's fine. But I did want to deal with some of the difficulties couples face when they really do want to have a lot of people join with them, but they feel totally overwhelmed by what it gets them into.

So, as you see, I'm putting the focus clearly on the wedding itself. This is what it's important to ask your guests to. It's up to you what you make of it. Your wedding can be a small, quiet affair, as you plan it. And you don't have to go far away – you can have a quiet wedding in your own parish.

'What if some of our guests are not Catholics?'
If there are to be guests of another faith, or of no faith, at your wedding, it would be good to mention this beforehand to the priest or minister who will assist you at the celebration, so he can be aware of it, and perhaps welcome them and help them follow the celebration more easily.

WHO WILL MARRY US?

The answer to that question is very simple. You marry one another. The priest or minister does not 'marry' you. In our Catholic tradition, you yourselves, the bride and groom, are the 'ministers of the sacrament' of marriage. It is you yourselves who, in your exchange of marriage vows, bring a blessing on one another. It is you yourselves who, all through your married life, bring a blessing on one another as you live out the life of love you begin on your wedding day. The person who assists you by officiating does not 'Pronounce you man and wife' after you exchange consent, as if that were necessary for the marriage to be true. The officiating minister simply receives your consent and prays that God will confirm the consent you have given, and may invite all present to express praise and thanks to God for this great moment of your lives.

The priest or minister who helps you by leading your celebration is an official witness, with the two other official witnesses, to what you do.

So who will it be? When the wedding is celebrated in the home parish of the bride (or groom), normally a priest of that parish will be available. Just as you need to check the availability of the church building, you need to check that he will be available for the day and time. Perhaps one of you has a relation or friend who is a priest or deacon, whom you would like to invite to assist at your celebration. Check his availability first, and then ask about this at the parish where the wedding is to take place, since he will need to be officially delegated for it. He himself could contact the parish directly to arrange this.

If you are planning your wedding in a parish other than the present home parish of either of you, they may welcome you to use the church building when available, but may ask that you arrange for whoever it is to assist you at your wedding. Don't presume this will be easy!

If you would like the assisting priest or minister at your wedding ceremony to join you afterwards at a wedding reception, you need to make this invitation clear.

YOUR PERSONAL PREPARATION

If you have not already done so, read the short sections near the beginning of the book: 'To the Bride and Groom', 'What Should We Do First?' and 'Countdown'.

Among the many things you may want to do to prepare for your wedding, there is a part of the preparation you may not think of. The way that your life is also your life in the Church can make the difference to how much at home you will feel in the church on your wedding day. You can feel at home, not just in the church building, but among the people who are the Church in your parish. They are a normal mixture of human beings, like anywhere else: not claiming to be better than anyone else, but wanting to live a better Christian life, a better life as followers of Jesus. Coming together to celebrate and pray each Sunday, we grow, hardly noticing it, as a community of people. I pray that the Church, your parish, is 'home' for you.

If either of you (or both of you) find you have drifted away from the Sunday celebration at your church, now is a good time to make a fresh start, as you come to a whole new phase of your lives – a phase that will be life-long. It can be really difficult, if it has not been part of your life for a long while; it takes time to let it become a natural part of your life again. Your wedding celebration will be so much more personal and enriching if it is not just a one-day event for you to come to the church, but part of the pattern of your life.

Even such a simple thing as being familiar with some of the forms of prayer we use will help a lot, rather than feeling like a fish out of water at your own wedding. If you go on holiday or honeymoon to a country where they use different money, you make sure you have the currency you need. The patterns of how we celebrate in church are like the 'currency' we use. If you have lost touch, you could begin now to know the currency, to learn the language, we use. Is your wedding worth it? Is it worth an hour a week from now until your wedding day?

There are people who have been deeply hurt and offended by something done by the Church or by some official of the Church. We know it should not happen, but it does. It's part of human life in every sphere, that people are hurt and offended. It is part of married life too – when two people live so close to one another, we can hardly help saying or doing something now and again that hurts the other person. At times it may even seem that we can do nothing right. The way to healing is not always easy. But if it is important to us, we can find it. We begin almost every celebration of Mass by asking forgiveness – we acknowledge that we fail. We also put our trust in the power of forgiveness and healing. If there is something which drove you away from the Church at some time, is there something you can do to find healing? It would be good to begin your married life, knowing healing in heart and soul, and in the various relationships in your life.

MAY I HAVE YOUR AUTOGRAPH?

What difference does a piece of paper make? Can we not just get married without all this?

When you buy a house or arrange a honeymoon, there are usually documents to prepare and sign. They are there to make sure everything is in order, and for the protection of every person involved. Life would be simpler if we could dispense with all that. But then it could also get very much more complicated. We know there's a good reason for it. It's the same when you plan to marry. Imagine if there were no way to know for sure who had married whom! Marriage and family are not just for the few people directly involved, but are a concern for the community, for society. That's why the communities of Church and State are involved.

I mentioned near the beginning of the book, in the section 'What Should We Do First?' on page 17, a little about what to do as you contact your parish and the State authority for registering marriage. Here, I would like just to say something about the procedures in Ireland.

You need to give at least three months' notice both to your parishes and to the local Registrar of Marriages. It's good to make contact six months or more in advance.

In Ireland the basic form, which one of the staff of your parish will go through with you, is called the Pre-Nuptial Enquiry. This may be revised from time to time; the details below are correct for the form as in use at the time of writing. The purpose of it is to help get everything in order before the wedding.

First of all, the Pre-Nuptial Enquiry form will need the basic information like your names and addresses, dates of birth, the date and time and place of the proposed wedding, and the person who will assist you by officiating at the ceremony. The form will help establish your freedom to marry. You may also be asked to provide a recent copy of a Certificate of your Baptism and of Confirmation. You can get these from the parish where you were baptised and confirmed. You will probably understand the reasons for the following questions – they are not meant to intimidate you. It is important that you understand what is asked. It is important, too, that you answer sincerely and truthfully and not just give an answer you think will get you by. It would be good to get together, just the two of you, beforehand, and discuss whatever significance the questions may have for your marriage.

> *Are you related to your proposed partner by blood or marriage or adoption?*
> *If you are a minor in civil law, have you followed the necessary procedures?*
> *Are you bound by religious vows or promises of celibacy?*
> *Have you ever contracted a religious or civil marriage?*
> *Have you any obligations arising from a previous union?*
> *For how long have you known your partner?*
> *When did the courtship begin?*
> *What marriage preparation have you undertaken?*
> *Are you entering marriage free from any kind of pressure from parents, fiancé(e) or anyone else?*
> *Do you intend to enter a permanent marriage that can be dissolved only by death?*
> *Do you accept that marriage involves a lifelong responsibility to love and support each other?*
> *Do you accept that being married means being faithful to each other for life?*
> *Do you understand and accept the rights and duties of marriage in relation to having and rearing children?*
> *Are you sure you are giving full consent to this marriage without reservation?*
> *Have you and your partner discussed married life seriously?*

In addition, all Catholics are asked the following:

> *Do you accept that marriage has been instituted by God and made a sacrament by Christ?*
> *Are you resolved to remain steadfast in your Catholic faith and to practise it regularly?*
> *Do you promise to do what you can within the unity of your partnership to have all the children of your marriage baptised and brought up in the Catholic faith?*

Doesn't all this make it sound a very serious and important matter? There would be something wrong if you were not serious about it – you're talking about how you want to live the rest of your life together. If you do not understand any of the questions, or if you have a problem about them, ask the person with whom you are completing the Pre-Nuptial Enquiry form.

When you have given your answers, you will be asked to sign your name to the answers you have given, signifying that the answers you have given are true. The priest will also sign it with you.

The Pre-Nuptial Enquiry form for each of you will be sent, along with any other papers that are needed, to the parish where the wedding will take place, and will be kept in the archives there.

PAPAL BLESSING

Some couples like to have a 'Papal Blessing' in time for the wedding. This is a decorative chart signed in Rome for the Pope, a symbol of his blessing and of the prayerful support of the whole Church. For this, ask a priest in your parish for a letter of recommendation, which you can then bring to a shop which will have a selection of patterns for you to choose from, and which will arrange the forwarding to Rome. (Veritas and other outlets provide this service. If you don't know where to find one, ask at your parish.) You would need to allow at least three months before the wedding if you want to be sure of having it back in time.

PASSPORTS

If you intend to go abroad on honeymoon immediately after the wedding, don't forget about your passports! If you already have a passport, check that it has not expired.

MONEY

It is amazingly simple to get married. You give yourself to one another in lifelong marriage before the official witnesses. That's all.

Because it is so simple many people surround the wedding with a lot of other items: things to help bring out the meaning of what they're doing, and to make a big celebration of it. Things like new clothes, and flowers, and cars, and a ring, and a reception, and a honeymoon. Try to remember what they mean. The one thing almost all of them have in common is that they cost money. Don't feel you have to have them all, or even any of them, just because everyone else seems to want them. You will probably be aware, too, that couples preparing for their wedding are often 'targeted' by commercial firms through publications, wedding fairs, direct marketing, etc. They can provide a valuable service. Just keep in mind that any purely commercial approach is less interested in your lifelong commitment to one another than in their opportunities for increasing profit by enticing you to spend more, or even in your lifelong commitment to their financial package.

Remember the meaning of what you are doing, and what it may mean to the people who may be there. Some things can take away from what the day means for you. Like making a big splash for fear of letting yourself down. On the other hand, things can help to really make the day if you keep your balance about them. Make up your own minds about each of the items, and ask the priest about the church side of it. Apart altogether from finding somewhere to live, among the items on which money goes at a wedding are:

Cake	Flowers	Photographs
Carpet	Honeymoon	Presents
Cars	Invitations	Ring(s)
Church	Music	Reception
Clothes	Papal blessing	Thank you notes

An offering is usually made to the parish. A parish depends on the contributions people offer, and needs them to continue the work of the parish in serving people and in helping to reach out to others. In order to do this, the contributions help in supporting those who work for the parish, and to maintain, repair, heat, light, clean, etc. Ask at the parish whether there is a policy in regard to offerings for weddings. Be assured that lack of money will never prevent anyone having their wedding in the church. However, it would seem strange if a couple spend large amounts of money on many other things to do with their wedding celebration, and make only a very small contribution to the parish and staff where the celebration is held. Consider the use of the church building and all that this involves, and the time taken by the priest or other minister in the preparation, administration and celebration; and the various other people involved. Taking all this into account, what contribution to your church do you think would be reasonable or generous? Compare it perhaps to what you may pay for the services of a professional photographer or florist who certainly can contribute to the occasion, but are not essential for the wedding.

An offering is usually made also to the sacristan who prepares the church, and to any parish altar-servers who may assist. If you have engaged other services that are quite separate from the parish – music, carpet, etc. – you need to make your own arrangements to pay for them.

To avoid confusion, it can help to put whatever contributions or payments you are making in envelopes clearly marked beforehand, and ask a reliable person to look after them.

PHOTOGRAPHS AND VIDEO

What is said here about photographs applies also to video.

You may decide for yourselves whether you want photographs of your wedding ceremony – it's not obligatory! The most important memento of your wedding will be the very life you live together, in the memory and continuation of what happened on your wedding day. Recording it other than in your lives and in the marriage register is a recent phenomenon, made possible by technology; it has advantages and disadvantages.

If you decide 'yes', decide then how to go about it. So many people nowadays have pocket cameras that it can be distracting if lights are flashing frequently. You may accept this, or you may prefer to ask that only one or two specified people take care of this matter.

It is important that a photographer at a wedding, whether professional or amateur, be discreet: the challenge is to photograph well without intruding or taking over; it is never good to interrupt the celebration just for the sake of a particular pose. The photographer will also need to know how the celebration is planned: for example, which way bride and groom will face as they give their consent to marry. The minister who assists at your wedding can be of help to you in planning this.

If you are paying a photographer to do this job, talk with him or her about which pictures you would like taken. An experienced photographer should be worth listening to. The final decision should be yours, keeping in mind what I have just said about being discreet. You can also decide how many pictures should be taken afterwards, and how much time to allow for them: they can occasionally become very tiresome!

REGISTERING YOUR MARRIAGE

The way that a wedding is registered with the civil authority (the government of the country) varies from country to country. The arrangement current in the Republic of Ireland is that the civil form is signed at the wedding by bride and groom, by the two official witnesses (who may be bridesmaid and best man for the ceremony, but not necessarily so), and by the priest or other minister who assists by officiating at the ceremony. Why not ask beforehand to see the form, so you'll know what it looks like?

Find out beforehand from the minister who will assist you at the wedding, or from a priest in the parish where the wedding will take place, whose responsibility it is to register the marriage with the civil authority.

See the Contacts section at the end of the book for information about applying for a Civil Certificate of Marriage. While you can get a church Certificate of Marriage right away from the parish where the wedding takes place, you may need a Civil Certificate of your marriage for various civil or State purposes. This will be available when the form you have signed has been sent in, and the information has been entered – it is not available immediately.

FLOWERS

If you are arranging for flowers to decorate the church, please consult one of the staff of the parish first. Moderation is good – we want people to be able to take part in the celebration without being distracted by the flowers. Usually it is best not to place flower arrangements where they will block the line of sight for people. At the altar, it is better to place flowers around it rather than on the altar. If any are placed on the altar, they need to be discreet, so that they will not be in the way. Remember, too, that people need room to move around.

DRESS

Dressing for a special occasion can add a lot to the celebration, and to your sense of occasion. Although many like to do so, it is not necessary to buy or hire a special set of clothes for your wedding day – some people like to dress in their 'Sunday Best', or to buy clothes they will be able to continue to wear on other occasions. Fashions do change, as you will know from seeing wedding photographs from many years ago. Keep in mind the kind of occasion it is, and choose what you will wear accordingly: that it is not a beach party or a fashion parade, but an important formal celebration and a religious event.

PART III

LOOKING AT THE CEREMONY

THE WEDDING CELEBRATION AND THE WEDDING MASS

In planning your church wedding, there is a decision whether to have the wedding celebration as an event in its own right, or to have the wedding celebration integrated with a celebration of Mass, a 'Nuptial Mass'. It is important to discuss it with the priest or other minister who will be officiating at your wedding. The word 'Liturgy' is used below to refer to the official church celebration.

When might it be appropriate to have the wedding celebration in its own right? For example, when:

a. you feel that the wedding celebration deserves to stand on its own, and you want to keep the focus of the celebration simple and direct;
b. you are members of different Churches, and you want both of you and all your guests to take full part in every aspect of the celebration;
c. one of you is not a baptised Christian;
d. there are some other circumstances in your situation or in that of many of your guests which indicate that this is your preferred option.

When might it be appropriate to have the wedding celebration integrated with a celebration of Nuptial Mass? For example, when:

a. you are members of the same Church, and Mass is an important and regular part of your lives, and will be a significant element at your wedding celebration and in your lives afterwards;
b. you are members of different Churches, but a celebration of Eucharist (also known as the Lord's Supper, or Holy Communion, or the Mass) is important in one or both of your lives, even though you may not be able to share fully in it on this day, due to the divisions that exist at present between the Churches;
c. there are some other circumstances in your situation or in that of many of your guests which indicate that this is your preferred option.

The following outlines give you a picture of each celebration. These may be useful to you as well in preparing a service leaflet for your guests.

Wedding Celebration – An outline of the celebration

Wedding Mass – An outline of the celebration

MAKE YOUR CHOICE!

Now, we look at the things that can go to make up the celebration of your wedding. Sometimes people have the impression that there is only one way to have a wedding, but in fact there are varying customs from different places and times. In the earlier parts of this book, you'll have looked at the more remote preparation for the ceremony. We will deal here only with the things directly related to the wedding celebration in the church: this is the wedding itself. The intention is to make it easier for you to choose the kind of celebration that will be most appreciated.

A celebration is a way of remembering something that is a cause of happiness for us, and a way of expressing that happiness. The remembering can be of the past – what has brought you to this moment; remembering the present moment as a gift to be lived with joy; and remembering the hopes and promises this moment holds for the future as you accept the call from God to live the gift of love in married life.

You know what you are about to do. No matter what other worries you may have, and no matter how distracted you may feel on the wedding day, your intention is clear. If you have made your choices about the ceremony, you will be much more a part of it. Even if things do not go exactly according to plan, this takes nothing from the wedding. In fact, the unplanned happenings of a well-planned day like this can make the day more memorable! You can plan all you like, and it's good to do so; but be always open to the possibility of surprises. So make your choices, and trust God to love you actively.

WAYS PEOPLE CAN SERVE

Everybody at a liturgical celebration, whether a normal service or a wedding, has a part to play: coming along, greeting one another, praying, listening, responding, singing, offering, receiving, going forth: how wholeheartedly they do these things will make a big difference to the 'feel' of the celebration. As well as this, quite a few people can be involved in special ways of serving: of 'ministering' in the celebration. Of course, one or two people could do nearly all of them, but it is far better if each person involved has just one ministry to perform.

1. **Ministers of the Sacrament of Marriage:** This way of ministering is one only the bride and groom can do: this is actually to marry each other! Nobody else – not even priest or registrar – can do this for you.
2. **Witnesses you will already have chosen:** the official witnesses for Church and State that you have married one another. Very often they are a man and woman whom we call 'best man' (odd title!) and 'bridesmaid'. But they may be any two people capable of witnessing. They could be two men or two women. They need not be members of your Church or of any Church. They stand with you as you exchange your consent, and they sign their names in the register to declare what they have witnessed. (If you have more groomsmen or bridesmaids, be clear on who you will ask to sign.) These witnesses usually make themselves available to help out with any other things that need to be looked after.
3. **Music:** See the following section about this.
4. **Art and flowers, etc.** The scope and need for this will depend on the actual building where the wedding takes place. Helps set an atmosphere of celebration. A lot of money could be spent, or it can be done tastefully on a minimum.
5. **Ushers/greeters** to make guests welcome – many will be in a strange church – and to show them to their places, give out leaflets (and pick them up after the wedding as well!) if necessary.
6. **Commentator** who gives explanations and instructions to the people so that they may be drawn into the celebration and better understand what is happening. Such interventions must be carefully prepared and kept short.
7. **Altar servers:** You may have some guests who serve or who used

to serve, or who would be willing to serve. They may be adults or children, male or female. It is not difficult, but they need to be prepared for this – they will need to know the plan of the celebration, so as to know how they serve at each part of the celebration. If you wish to have altar servers and have none from among your guests, the parish where you are celebrating your wedding may be able to arrange it.

8. **Readers** who proclaim the Word of God in Scripture. Don't just ask people to do this to honour them: it is important that the message be communicated well. They need preparation – make sure they have a copy of what they are to read a week ahead; it is difficult to read intelligently if you are only asked as you come into the church! The reading needs to speak first of all to the reader, in order to be able to convey it effectively to others. Dead words on a page need to become words of life. If possible, arrange for the Responsorial Psalm to be sung: it is a song, and loses a lot if just spoken. A Veritas publication, *Readings for your Wedding,* edited by Brian Magee CM, would be useful to readers. (More about the readings themselves on page 106.)
9. **Prayer of the Faithful:** These should be prepared and led not by an ordained minister, but by one or more lay persons. Just as for reading the Word of God, preparation is necessary. There are sample prayers on pages 180-83; this is exactly what they are: samples, to be adapted or substituted. Bride and groom could prepare them and ask a guest to lead them; or you could ask a guest to prepare them. See the guidelines on page 180.
10. **Preparation of the gifts and of the altar:** people to bring forward the bread and wine, and any other item required to prepare the altar for the Liturgy of the Eucharist. The number of people depends on what you want to arrange. Talk it over with the minister involved. If there are other items of symbolic significance that you would like brought forward for the celebration, this is done at the start of the ceremony. The preparation of the gifts and of the altar concerns only those items that are used during the Liturgy of the Eucharist.

11. **Ministers of the Eucharist** to assist in the distribution of Holy Communion. If there is a commissioned minister among your guests, you may like him or her to assist. Arrange this with a priest of the parish where the wedding will take place. Alternatively, you could invite one of the ministers of the Eucharist from the parish itself.

MUSIC

Some people like a quiet wedding; others like to add an extra air of celebration to it by having music. How you plan this depends first of all on the occasion itself: the wedding is a liturgical celebration, and music has a very definite and clear part to play in this. Within this, there is a wide choice, which will depend on your decision, on the musical resources available, and on the people who will be at the wedding.

Where there is music in the celebration, it has a more important place than is sometimes realised. It is not there just to provide beautiful sounds and/or words and to help create an atmosphere, although I hope it would also do this. When we use music during a Church celebration, it is not just background; nor is it a performance. It is part of the worship and prayer: it is an integral part of the celebration. It will help not just to create the atmosphere of the celebration; it will also help to unite all who are there in prayer and praise.

So what kind of music do you want to look for? There are many different styles of church music: hymns we remember since childhood, Gregorian chant, traditional and folk hymns, classical, and perhaps others you may think of. Whatever your preferred style, the question to ask is: 'Does it express our faith in God and in Jesus Christ?' There may be many beautiful love songs that bring a tear to your eyes, which are 'Our song!', or which you have seen or heard at other weddings or in films or television. There may be songs that express a beautiful and inspiring philosophy of life. How can you decide whether to use these at the wedding ceremony in the church, or at the wedding reception, or some other occasion? For our celebration, our worship in the church, ask yourselves the question above: 'Does it express our faith in God and in Jesus Christ?'

In choosing the music for your church wedding, you will want to consult together, along with the officiating priest or other minister, and the person or persons who will lead us in the music area of the celebration. It is good to have musicians who are familiar with music at the liturgy – they may have extra suggestions, and will be more likely to know what is appropriate. It does not have to be all 'wedding

Others like to add an extra air of celebration by having music...

music' – other music for liturgical celebrations is also good, and may be well known. Before you make final decisions on the music, make sure that the officiating priest or other minister has a list of the full programme. It is a good idea to ask whoever is leading the music to contact the officiating priest or minister, especially if they are not part of the music ministry in the parish where the wedding is to take place.

First of all, think how you could encourage your guests to sing. Difficult? But would you have much difficulty if you are having a reception afterwards? If you don't see how you can achieve it, ask the person(s) who will be looking after the music for suggestions on how to bring it about.

A solo singer has often tended to be just that: a solo singer, and sometimes singing pieces that are beautiful and frequently associated with weddings, but that are not really very suitable for liturgy. It would be much more valuable for a good celebration to have a soloist (or a few singers) to act as 'cantor'. That would mean *leading the people in song,* for example, in the Responsorial Psalm where the people have a short refrain to sing; and to lead them also in the Gospel Acclamation (the 'Alleluia', except during Lent), in the Holy, Holy, the Memorial Acclamation after the Consecration, and the Great Amen.

Similarly, the first function of a choir at a liturgy is not performance, but to lead and encourage the congregation to sing. After that, the soloist or choir may also sing without the people at certain parts of the liturgy.

If you give your guests the words and some encouragement, you'll often find them happy to be able to take part more actively. What their voices are like does not make a great difference; singing in church is not something only for singers; it is for all believers! There could be a short rehearsal with those who come for the wedding practice; a group of friends would be friends indeed if they would practise beforehand so as to be able to lead the rest.

Two practical points

1. The 'Our Father' should not be sung so as to exclude the congregation; if they cannot join in singing it, it is better spoken.
2. Ensure that it is possible for the musician(s) to receive Communion at the appropriate time in the celebration.

ARRANGING THINGS IN THE CHURCH

At your wedding, you will have a different position and part to take in the celebration to how you would more usually attend a celebration, because you, the couple who are about to marry, will be the ministers of the sacrament of marriage to one another. Also, ask what people have a specific role to play, and where they need to be. If there are musicians, where will they lead from? For a wedding Mass, where will the bread and wine and other requisites be?

Churches differ in size and layout, so you'll want to check what are the normal positions for the bride and groom, and for witnesses during the wedding. You may prefer to be in front of the altar, and facing it; or you may prefer to be at the side (for example, bride and groom on one side and witnesses on the other, to avoid having your backs to people), and then come together in the centre for the ceremony of consent.

Then you might like to ask the priest if he could arrange a practice some time in the week before the wedding. It can help you to feel more relaxed on the wedding day itself.

OTHER IDEAS AND CUSTOMS

There are many variations possible within the actual shape of the ceremony and within the liturgy of Mass, as you see it above, and as you will see in detail in Part IV; make full use of the possibilities offered there. For example, the special Irish language rite on page 175 (translation on page 247) is significantly different; look at the final Solemn Blessing with the Cross of St Brigid, which the priest then presents to the couple; look also at the Solemn Calling and the Prayer of the Faithful.

Various people and places add other ideas to the ceremony in order to enhance the celebration. These can be helpful and attractive; but if you add too many such elements, the 'trimmings' can obscure what is central. You may have observed such ideas in practice at other weddings; consider carefully what may or may not be valuable in yours.

One such symbol is popular: the wedding candle. At a pre-arranged stage of the celebration after they exchange their consent, the newly-married couple light a candle in the sanctuary as a symbol of the united married life they have just started. It may be on the altar, or in some other place; it is important that it be clearly visible, and that what the bride and groom are doing is visible. The simplest way is to do it in silence, perhaps after a word of commentary. Sometimes a couple have two other candles which they light at the beginning of the celebration – they may be lit from the Paschal Candle, as a symbol of the life they began at their Baptism. If you have the candles used at your own Baptisms, you could use these (it doesn't matter if they do not match). Then, after the exchange of vows or another pre-arranged time, you light the wedding candle from those two candles. But don't extinguish the first two candles – we hope your Baptism is still very much alive! I suggest that if you do want to light one or more candles on the altar, you go around to the other side of the altar to do so. In this way, all the people you invited will be able to see what you're doing. Some wedding candles are commercially available; or you could get a simple candle of your choice, and put it in a holder and decorate it with a few small flowers and suitable marriage and Christian symbols. A single thick candle with two wicks can sometimes be got. Some may even be able to make their own candle. Your wedding candle could then be lit at home on special occasions like your wedding anniversary.

Other customs that have been used in Christian weddings at different times and places are:

Simple 'crowns' for bride and groom.
Anointing of the bride and groom.
Putting a veil over both bride and groom together.
Presentation of a Bible to the couple as a sign of their way of life.
Witnesses or other members of the congregation 'laying hands' on the couple at the Nuptial Blessing.
Blessing of bread (not the Eucharist – perhaps the cake?) to be shared by all after the wedding.
Bride and groom saying a word of welcome to the guests whom they themselves have invited, immediately after the opening of the celebration.
Having the 'Examination' at the very start of the wedding Mass, and preparing your own in consultation with the minister involved (see sample on page 255).
Including a short form of asking the Church, as represented by the assembled guests, to promise their continued support.
A short formula to be said by the person receiving the ring.
A joyful song immediately after the Liturgy of Marriage.

Where they are not already provided for in the rite, they can be specially arranged.

In addition, the Liturgy of the Word and of the Eucharist provide possibilities of which people are often not aware. For example:

Fuller entrance procession.
Incense.

Enthroning of Bible.
Blessing and sprinkling of water at start.
Sung scripture readings.
Short pause for reflection after readings, homily, marriage, Communion.
Sung prayer of the faithful and response.
Preparing and providing the eucharistic bread and wine.
Fuller preparation of altar for Liturgy of the Eucharist.
Sung 'dialogue' at start of Eucharistic Prayer.
Sung Preface and Eucharistic Prayer.
Extra acclamations sung in Eucharistic Prayer.

All these would need to be discussed with the people concerned in planning the celebration. Just remember not to overload the occasion!

PART IV

THE CEREMONY

PLANNING YOUR ARRIVAL

The first thing to do is to arrive! One common way for doing this is that the groom arrives ten or fifteen minutes early with the best man, bringing ring(s), gift(s), leaflets if used, envelopes with offerings, etc., and waits for the bride to arrive. There is, however, no reason why you could not arrive together if you wish, and come in arm in arm, without being given away.

But, before each of you leaves for the church, how about a little time out?

> *Most loving Father,*
> *I thank you for what you are about to do for us at our wedding.*
> *I thank you for N. whom I'm about to marry.*
> *I thank you for bringing us together in love.*
> *Be with us right now, and with everyone coming to the wedding.*
> *May your Spirit of love fill us now in mind and heart, in body and soul.*
> *Unite us in your love now and forever. Amen.*

(Of *COURSE* I'm crazy – who would *EVER* have time to pray before their wedding?)

Decide whether you want to be 'given away' – formally separating from parents and family, to come to one another. People usually think this is just of the bride, by her father. Again, there is no reason why it should not be of both bride and groom, and it could be done by either or both parents of each. It could be at the door of the church, with friends and officiating minister gathered around; all could then come up the church in procession singing the opening hymn together. Alternatively, this formal leave-taking could take place just in front of the altar; it could take place as soon as you arrive, or it could be at the start of the Liturgy of Marriage, after the readings.

However you plan your arrivals at the church, in deference to the importance of the occasion and in courtesy to your guests and the staff of the church, you should arrive *in good time.* Of course,

There would be nothing wrong with both of you arriving together.

unforeseen snags may arise to delay one or other; but take at least normal care to be on time, as you would for any other important event.

Anyone who is serving the celebration – readers, etc. – and who is not familiar with the church should arrive early to see to whatever is needed. In a large church, guests who are strangers may scatter down the church; have someone encourage them to come closer together, and it will make for a better atmosphere.

Phrases throughout the ceremony which are identified as (*) may be omitted in particular cases – for example, if the couple are advanced in years.

INTRODUCTORY RITE

There may be an entrance song.
If there is no song or music, then you may choose an entrance antiphon as a short meditation to help set the scene for the celebration. Choose A, B or C:

A
Ps 19:3,5
May the Lord send you help from his holy place and from Zion may he watch over you. May he grant you your heart's desire and lend his aid to all your plans.

B
Ps 89:14,17
Fill us with your love, O Lord, and we will sing for joy all our days. May the goodness of the Lord be upon us, and give success to the work of our hands.

C
Ps 114:2,9
Lord, I will bless you day after day, and praise your name for ever; for you are kind to all and compassionate to all your creatures.

All begin by making the sign of the cross together: the sign of God's love for us. Then the priest greets everyone. He may use one of the following greetings:

A	B	C
Priest: The grace of our Lord Jesus Christ and the love of God and the Fellowship of the Holy Spirit be with you all.	The grace and peace of God our Father and the Lord Jesus Christ be with you.	The Lord be with you.
All: And also with you.	And also with you. *or* Blessed be God, the Father of our Lord Jesus Christ.	And also with you.

The priest can now introduce the Mass to help people to know how it has been planned and to put the bride and groom at ease!

See also alternative opening address on page 255.

PENITENTIAL RITE

We now have the Penitential Rite – we admit that we don't always succeed in loving others the way we should and we ask forgiveness. Love is tested when one person hurts another; both can show the strength of their love by asking pardon or by forgiving. We first take a few moments to remember our weaknesses; and then we ask pardon. There are three normal forms:

A	B	C
All: I confess to almighty God, and to you, my brothers and sisters, that I have sinned, through my own fault,	*P:* Lord, we have sinned against you: *All:* Lord, have mercy.	*P:* You were sent to heal the contrite: Lord, have mercy. *All:* Lord, have mercy.
in my thoughts	*P:* Lord, show us	*P:* You came to

and in my words,
in what I have done,
and in what I have
failed to do;
and I ask blessed
Mary, ever virgin,
all the angels and saints,
and you, my brothers
and sisters, to pray
for me to the Lord
our God.

your mercy and love.
All: And grant us
your salvation.

call sinners:
Christ, have mercy.
All: Christ, have mercy.

P: You plead for
us at the right
hand of the Father:
Lord, have mercy.
All: Lord, have mercy.

If you choose the third Penitential Rite, different forms may be composed. Each form of Penitential Rite continues with:

P: May almighty God have mercy on us,
forgive us our sins,
and bring us to everlasting life.
All: Amen.

The 'Lord, have mercy' *follows form A and B.*

The Rite of Blessing and Sprinkling of Holy Water may replace the complete Penitential Rite, as a renewal of our Baptism.

The Gloria may be said or sung, praising God for the blessings of this day.

Glory to God in the highest,
and peace to his people on earth.
Lord, God, heavenly King,
almighty God and Father,
we worship you, we give you thanks,
we praise you for your glory.

Lord Jesus Christ, only Son of the Father,
Lord God, Lamb of God,

you take away the sin of the world:
have mercy on us;
you are seated at the right hand of the Father:
receive our prayer.

For you alone are the Holy One,
you alone are the Lord,
you alone are the most high,
Jesus Christ,
with the Holy Spirit,
in the glory of God the Father. Amen.

Opening Prayer

Everyone is now invited to pray in silence for some moments. This is followed by a prayer. (You have a choice of four.) Whichever prayer you choose, it will be made through our Lord, Jesus Christ, the greatest witness to God's love the world has known.

A

This recalls that married love is a reminder of Christ's love for his people and prays that your love may be as wholehearted as his.

Father,
you have made the bond of marriage
a holy mystery,
a symbol of Christ's love for his Church.
Hear our prayers for *(both your names)*.
With faith in you and in each other
they pledge their love today.
May their lives always bear witness
to the reality of that love.

B

This prayer recalls that God made husband and wife to be one in love and asks that your love may grow and be inspiring to others.

Father,
when you created mankind
you willed that man and wife should be one.
Bind *(names)* in the loving union of marriage
and make their love fruitful
so that they may be living witnesses
to your divine love in the world.

C

This simply asks that God will strengthen your love.

Father,
hear our prayers for *(both your names)*,
who today are united in marriage before your altar.
Give them your blessing,
and strengthen their love for each other.

D

This is a prayer that your marriage will bring a blessing on the whole Church.

Almighty God,
hear our prayers for *(names)*,
who have come here today
to be united in the sacrament of marriage.
Increase their faith in you and in each other,
and through them bless your Church
(*with Christian children).

LITURGY OF THE WORD

The 'Liturgy of the Word' is where we have readings from the Bible.

Very strange, isn't it? Why would anyone want to include stories and writings which are 2000 or more years old into their wedding celebration today?

Of course, some parts of the Bible are very comforting and beautiful. Maybe there's a reading you've heard so often at weddings that you wouldn't feel properly married without it! But then there are other parts of the Bible that are difficult and disturbing and challenging. As you look at readings from the Bible, look for both sides in each reading: the side that expresses the beauty and wonder of what you're doing, and the side that invites you to a deeper and fuller life as you begin your marriage. At the end of this book, there's an Appendix: 'Introducing the Bible' (p. 274), which you may find helpful.

The Bible has had a special place among Christians over the past 2000 years. You are probably familiar with many parts of the Bible which you have heard over the years. You hear stories of the birth of Jesus in many ways every Christmas. You'll find the original stories of this in the first two chapters of St Matthew's Gospel and St Luke's Gospel.

The amazing thing is that people over the years have found that some parts of the Bible speak to them in a very special way. The Bible is really a collection of books, all put together into one. The Bible as we use it in the Catholic Church has some extra parts in the 'Old Testament' (the part from before the time of Jesus) not included in the Bible as used by some other Churches, but we agree on most. The 'New Testament' has the writings from after the time of Jesus: these include the four Gospels (accounts of the life of Jesus), and various other letters and writings. Below, you'll see how you can make your choices of readings.

What we read at this part of the wedding celebration is always from the Bible. The Bible was written in two languages – Hebrew and Greek, and has been translated many times into English and Irish and many other languages. Even in the same language, there are many ways to translate the same thought. If you have a Bible at home, you can look at some of these readings, and see how similar they are, and how they differ in some ways. The readings given here are from a translation into English called the New Jerusalem Bible, *which was published in 1985. The Responsorial Psalms (one of these follows the first reading) are from the* Grail *translation. There are many other good translations available in English, Irish, and other languages. If you don't have a Bible yourselves, why not give yourselves a wedding gift of one now – or if you have a gift-list, even include it on that.*

Not all the readings given here speak explicitly about marriage – you are recommended to include at least one reading which does explicitly refer to marriage. There may be some other reading from the Bible, not included here, which you would like to consider for your wedding. If you cannot find where it is in the Bible, one of the staff of your parish may be able to help.

Each reading has a section 'About the Reading'. This does not try to tell you what meaning you should get from the reading. Rather, it tries to provide some ideas for you to 'chew' over the reading, and so get your own 'nourishment' from it. I've tried not to make it more difficult!

When you have each had a chance to pick out some readings, it would be good to take some time over them to make the final selection. You could each read over a reading, marking any word or phrase that strikes you, or puzzles you, or challenges you; and talk about these together. You don't have to have the same understanding of the reading – it's more important to share your different understandings, and so come to know one another better. Then see if you can put in one or two sentences what it seems the reading is saying to each of you.

Couples sometimes ask about using readings from other sources. Any such reading would need to be suitable for a place in our worship, and does not replace the readings from the Bible. Some such readings could be suitably used at another part of the celebration – perhaps as a meditation or a prayer. Discuss this with the priest or other minister involved in the celebration. In this book, we just deal with the readings from the Bible.

Here God speaks to you and to all of us, and gives us wisdom for living. There is a wide selection of readings from the Bible for weddings. Each reading gives some insight into an aspect of love or marriage. Each reading given here is followed by a reflection on its meaning. The choice is yours! There are many other readings in the Bible that you may like to look at. If you are celebrating your wedding in one of the special seasons like Christmas or Easter, you may like to include a reading for the season – ask the priest or other minister who will officiate. Here are some other suggestions:

Old Testament:
Ezekiel 36:24-28: A new heart and a new spirit
Isaiah 43:1-2a: Be not afraid
Isaiah 61:10-11: I exult for joy
Ruth 1:16-17: Wherever you go, I shall go
Sirach (Ecclesiasticus) 6:14-17: A friend beyond price

New Testament:
1 Corinthians 12:12-13: We are baptised into one body
1 Peter 2:4-10: You are a chosen race
Ephesians 6:10-18: Grow strong in the Lord
Galatians 3:26-28: We are all one in Christ Jesus
Galatians 5:16-25: The fruit of the Spirit is love, joy, peace
Romans 6:3-11: We live a new life
Romans 8:26-32: God works with all who love him

Gospel:
Mark 10:13-16: To such as these belongs the kingdom
Mark 12:28-34: Love is more important than any sacrifice
Luke 18:15-17: To such belongs the kingdom
Luke 24:13-35: They recognised him at the breaking of bread
John 3:1-8: Those born from above
John 3:16-17: God so loved the world
John 6:44-47: Everyone who believes has eternal life
John 7:37-39: Streams of living water welling up
John 15:1-11: Abide in me, as I in you

You may have either two or three readings arranged like this:

*(a) Old Testament reading,
followed by a psalm,
which is prayer or meditation
in reply to the reading.*

(b) New Testament reading.

*(c) Gospel acclamation, followed
by Gospel reading.*

Or

*(a) Old Testament or
New Testament reading,
followed by a psalm in reply.*

*(b) Gospel acclamation
followed by Gospel reading.*

Some of your guests at the wedding may be regular readers in their parishes. You may like to ask them to undertake a reading; or you may like to ask other people. In any case, it is important that a person reading has a chance to prepare, so as to be able to communicate effectively. It is not a performance, but part of our worship together, so a person reading should be someone for whom their faith in Jesus Christ is important. A reader should know to speak clearly, not too fast, so that people can hear and understand.

A reader could perhaps come to the rehearsal for the wedding, to be familiar with the location, and take part in the practice. It is good for the reader to make eye-contact with those present at the celebration – perhaps when announcing: 'A reading from…'. Again at the end, the reader can look up and say 'The Word of the Lord!' or 'This is the Word of the Lord!' All reply: 'Thanks be to God!'

It is good to arrange with readers to allow a short pause – even just ten or fifteen seconds – after a reading before going on to the next part. It helps people have a chance to absorb what they've heard. After all, isn't that why you choose the reading?

You can also choose a suitable reading from one of the Gospels for the priest or deacon to read at the wedding.

With each reading given below, there is a short introduction at the beginning (not to be read aloud), and each reading is also accompanied by some suggestions as to how the reading may speak to you.

The Bible was written by human beings. Some of their names we know, some we don't. But as you read, just remember that they are saying something very important. Sometimes, when you talk together, one of you may be saying something really important to you both, but the other may not always realise it. The secret is to listen with your heart as well as with your head. You're not just listening to ideas or words, but to a person. It's the same with these readings.

You see, as Christians, we believe that God speaks to us; it's not just talking at God and hoping that he hears but never really knowing. We believe that God can speak to us through people. God can touch our lives through the people we love and through people in authority and through anyone at all. He speaks to us in the Bible through people he guided by the Holy Spirit; even people who may have thought at the time that they were just speaking for themselves, but whom we have come to realise that God was using to speak to us.

The Old Testament readings and psalms come from the time before Christ and have many beautiful thoughts. The psalms are prayers. We use the responsorial psalm for meditation after the first reading; the response gives a central thought to focus on. There are 150 psalms altogether in every edition of the Bible; but in some Bibles you may find a difference of one or two in the

The important thing for the reader is to know what the reading is trying to say.

numbering for many psalms, because of a different way of dividing them. The New Testament readings (including Gospel readings) come from the life of the first Christians.

The whole Bible is made up of many books, stories, poems, prayers, advice, letters, prophecies. Each book is divided into short chapters (a few very short books have only one chapter) and each chapter is divided into verses – a sentence or two, or part of a sentence, at a time. That means that no matter what Bible you have, you can usually find the piece if you have the name of the book and the number of the chapter and verse.

Old Testament Readings

1. A reading from the book of Genesis (1:26-28, 31a)

(This tells us that human life comes from God and that everything about it is good. Love is an image of God's goodness.)

God said, 'Let us make man in our own image, in the likeness of ourselves, and let them be masters of the fish of the sea, the birds of heaven, the cattle, all the wild animals and all the creatures that creep along the ground.'

God created man in the image of himself, in the image of God he created him, male and female he created them.

God blessed them, saying to them, 'Be fruitful, multiply, fill the earth and subdue it. Be masters of the fish of the sea, the birds of heaven and all the living creatures that move on earth.'

God saw all he had made, and indeed it was very good.

About the reading: The image of your father

Think how much the world has changed since the time your father and mother were your age: new inventions and discoveries; so many things not there any more; changes in the city and countryside; changes in the way people live and think and work and pray.

One of the things that has been changing is the use of the word 'man'. It was normally used in two senses: 'man' in the sense of 'a male person', and 'man' in the sense of 'a human being', or 'the human race'. The well-known book by Charles Darwin which he called The Descent of Man *uses the word in this last sense. You will find it used in this sense too in the Bible; usually, it will be clear which meaning is the intended one.*

Men and women have changed the world so much – we have power to change it. That's what this reading means by 'He made us in his image and likeness'. Of course it's something that doesn't come easily – we have to work at it. This is our special responsibility from God.

We human beings have sometimes taken 'subdue' to mean approval for exploiting and plundering and destroying both the world we live in and our fellow human beings. We need to learn how to exercise true responsibility. The love and care and reverence of a man and woman for one another in marriage can teach us a lot. We have been used to associating the word 'God' with a male personality – in order to speak of a 'person' in the English language, we have to use either 'he' or 'she'. But here, and in other places in the Bible, it is clear that what we would often think of as female characteristics are attributed to God. Can you try to think of God as personifying all that is good and wonderful in what we associate with both women and men? Then go beyond that, to realise that whatever way we think or speak of God, the reality of what God is is far beyond anything we can say or think.

In this Bible story, human life is presented as the high point of God's creation, the climax of the whole work. We, male and female, body and soul, sexuality and all, are made in God's image and likeness. Can you look at all the people in your life and see them in that light? Can you look at one another, and see one another as a reminder, an embodiment of God's goodness?

The work of being masters of the earth is a blessing from God; so is the life that you're planning to take on now – the bringing of new lives into the world. This is a work to be carried out responsibly and it's a blessing. Some people have thought that there's something bad about our bodies and sex and having children. It's quite clear in this reading that these are good and that they are from God. There are other possible ways that new life might come about: for instance, by one human being splitting into two, like some tiny living creatures do; or by taking a seed or slip from a person, like with a plant, and letting it grow in the ground. But the way that God chose in his love is by a man and woman coming together in love. Think how different your life would be if it wasn't like that!

Your coming together and your living together is something you have to work at. It takes effort, patience, courage, and most of all, love. That's true both before the wedding and afterwards, all your married life.

About the story of creation, in this reading and the next one: it's not history, as if there were a reporter there to cover it all and write about it. It's the basic facts of life – why the world exists, what our place in the world is; that nothing in the world is a god, but that all comes from the one God, including man and woman and their sexual life; that there is evil in the world; that sin comes from our not accepting God's plan, but that God still loves us and wants to save us.

About the sin of Adam and Eve: You'll find this story in chapter 3 of the book of Genesis, at the beginning of the Bible. The story is not 'history' in the sense we use the word nowadays: as an exact historical account of what happened when, as a television camera might have recorded it. Rather, it is meant to help us understand the facts of history. So we can't say that the sin was any one definite sin that we can name, like, for instance, stealing an apple. Neither can we say that it was sexual intercourse as if there was something bad about that in itself; in fact, this reading makes it quite clear that sexual intercourse has a very good and necessary place in God's plan. We can say that what is wrong is a part of every sin, whether stealing or murder or adultery or any other sin; it's a refusal to work with God.

2. A reading from the book of Genesis (2: 18-24)

(This reading tells us that man and woman belong naturally to one another – we're all of the one flesh, all equal.)

The Lord God said, 'It is not right that the man should be alone. I shall make him a helper.' So from the soil the Lord God fashioned all the wild animals and all the birds of heaven. These he brought to the man to see what he would call them; each one was to bear the name the man would give it. The man gave names to all the cattle, all the birds of heaven and all the wild animals. But no helper suitable for the man was found for him. Then, the Lord God made the man fall into a deep sleep. And, while he was asleep, he took one of his ribs and closed the flesh up again forthwith. The Lord God fashioned the rib he had taken from the man into a woman, and brought her to the man. And the man said: 'This one at last is bone of my bones and flesh of my flesh! She is to be called Woman, because she was taken from Man.' This is why a man leaves his father and mother and becomes attached to his wife, and they become one flesh.

About the reading: A team of two

Sometimes you might feel you'd like to go away and live just on your own on a deserted island; but everyone knows what it's like to feel lonely. After reading seven times in chapter 1 of the book of Genesis that 'God saw that it was good' we now come to 'The Lord God said: It is NOT good that the man should be alone'. And to emphasise the importance of what God did, the writer tells a story of the making of all the animals and birds, but none of them would do. What man needed was someone of the same nature as himself.

Man and woman are completely of the same nature: 'bone from my bones and flesh from my flesh'. But man and woman are not completely the same. If they are 'helpers', each helps the other out with whatever abilities and gifts each has. You are two different kinds of people. You can be learning now how you are different: how you think differently, feel differently, love differently and develop differently from each other. You want to know one another as you really are, so there should be no need to pretend with one another – to put on a false face. Look your best, act your best but not falsely. Living together, it's hard not to be your natural self and it's your natural selves right here and now that you want to love and be helper to.

The punch-line of this reading comes at the very end – what the story has been leading up to. 'Helper' means a lot. One body means a lot more. For a man, getting married doesn't mean going to another home where he'll be the boss, and where he'll have all the comforts of home without having to do what he's told and with the added bonus of sex. For a woman, it's not going to another home where she'll be secure and be able to organise things as she wants them, and live happily ever after right from the start.

There is, of course, a certain amount of truth in these; but most important of all, it means that they become one body, giving their lives for one another. 'The greatest love anyone can have for another person is to lay down his life for a friend', is what Jesus said.

As you're thinking about this, spare some thoughts for those who do not marry, for whatever reason, and for widows and widowers and others on their own. They can sometimes experience a deep loneliness. Any time, too, that you feel cut off from one another in any way and know the loneliness of it, remember that it's your very closeness that can make the loneliness seem so bad, and at the same time makes it bearable and gives you reason to overcome it. Lastly, remember in particular those who do not marry 'for the sake of the kingdom of heaven' – those who choose a different way to show their love in serving God and his people.

3. A reading from the book of Genesis (24:48-51, 58-69)
(This story tells how God's hand was seen in arranging a marriage between Isaac and Rebekah.)

Abraham's servant said to Laban: 'I bowed down and worshipped the Lord, and I blessed the Lord, God of my master Abraham, who had led me by a direct path to choose the daughter of my master's brother for his son. Now tell me whether you are prepared to show constant and faithful love to my master; if not, say so, and I shall know what to do.' Laban and Bethuel replied, 'This is from the Lord; it is not for us to say yes or no to you. Rebekah is there before you. Take her and go; and let her become the wife of your master's son, as the Lord has decreed.' They called Rebekah and asked her, 'Will you go with this man?' She replied, 'I will.' Accordingly they let their sister Rebekah go, with her nurse, and Abraham's servant and his men. They blessed Rebekah and said to her: 'Sister of ours, from you may there spring thousands and tens of thousands! May your descendants gain possession of the gates of their enemies!'

And forthwith, Rebekah and her maids mounted the camels, and followed the man. The servant took Rebekah and departed. Isaac meanwhile had come back from the well of Lahai Roi and was living in the Negeb. While Isaac was out walking towards evening in the fields, he looked up and saw camels approaching. And Rebekah looked up and saw Isaac. She jumped down from her camel, and asked the servant, 'Who is that man walking through the fields towards us?' The servant replied, 'That is my master.' So she took her veil and covered herself up. The servant told Isaac the whole story. Then Isaac took her into his tent. He married Rebekah and made her his wife. And in his love for her, Isaac was consoled for the loss of his mother.

***About the reading:* Love story**
If someone 2000 years hence were to read about how the two of you came to get married, it might sound as strange to them as the story of Isaac and Rebekah does to us. We have just part of it here; the whole story takes up all of chapter 24 of the

book of Genesis. Abraham had left his own country long before; now that his son Isaac is grown up, he sends his servant back home to find a wife for Isaac. The servant in fact comes on some relations of Abraham. Behind the whole story is the belief that God has been guiding the people involved. This is the point of the story, even though the people themselves don't always realise it. For instance, Rebekah's brother Laban is probably more interested in Abraham's wealth than in his sister's marriage! The goodbye blessing that Rebekah's family spoke wouldn't be common nowadays, but is an echo of God's promise to Abraham that his descendants would become a great nation. The warlike bit reflects the times they lived in.

If you're planning that the bride comes into the church with a veil over her face, you can see here how old a custom it is: a bride of the time was not allowed to let the bridegroom see her face before the wedding.

A husband and wife strike out on their own when they marry; they make a new life together. It can take some time for them to centre their lives on one another. It doesn't mean they should forget to love their own parents. These are two different kinds of love – it's important not to mix them up. And a husband and wife can bring great consolation and healing to one another, as Isaac discovered. You share your sorrows and joys: as we say – 'for better, for worse; for richer, for poorer; in sickness and in health'. The fact that the match between Isaac and Rebekah was arranged according to the custom of the times did not mean that they did not love one another.

4. A reading from the book of Tobit (7:6-14)

(This tells us the story of how Raguel, Sarah's father, came to give her hand in marriage to her cousin Tobias, and prayed that God would bless them. In this reading, the word 'sister' can also mean 'cousin' or 'wife'.)

Raguel said to Tobias, 'Blessings on you, child! You are the son of a noble father. How sad it is that someone so bright and full of good deeds should have gone blind!' He fell on the neck of his kinsman Tobias and wept. And his wife Edna wept for him, and so did his daughter Sarah. Raguel killed a ram from the flock, and they gave them a warm welcome.

They washed and bathed and sat down to table. Then Tobias said to Raphael, 'Brother Azarias, will you ask Raguel to give me my sister Sarah?' Raguel overheard the words, and said to the young man, 'Eat and drink, and make the most of your evening; no one else has the right to take my daughter Sarah, no one but you, my brother. In any case even I am not at liberty to give her to anyone else, since you are her next of kin. However, my boy, I must be frank with you: I have tried to find a husband for her seven times among our kinsmen, and all of them have died the first evening, on going to her room. But for the present, my boy, eat and drink; the Lord will grant you his grace and peace.' Tobias spoke out, 'I will not hear of eating and drinking till you have come to a decision about me.' Raguel answered, 'Very well. Since, by the prescription of the Book of Moses she is given to you, heaven itself decrees she shall be yours. I therefore entrust your sister to you. From now on you are her brother and she is your sister. She is given to you from today for ever. The Lord of heaven favour you tonight, my child, and grant you his grace and peace.'

Raguel called for his daughter Sarah, took her by the hand and gave her to Tobias with these words, 'I entrust her to you; the law and the ruling recorded in the Book of Moses assign her to you as your wife. Take her; bring her home safe and sound to your father's house. The God of heaven grant you a good journey in peace.' Then he turned to her mother and asked her to fetch him writing paper. He drew up the marriage contract, and so he gave his daughter as bride to Tobias according to the ordinance of the Law of Moses. After this they began to eat and drink.

About the reading: Made in heaven

Here and in the next reading we get a look at another strange love story. Again, it's not history, although the writer uses the names of places and people that did exist. You could read the whole story yourselves in the Bible.

(This book is not included in some Bibles. We haven't got it in its original language, but in translations. It has, however, been used by the Church from early times.)

One thing stands out in the part of the story we take in this reading: that heaven is very much a part of our life story here on earth. It says twice that the wedding is according to the Law of God (as in the book of Moses); it says, too, that heaven decrees the wedding of Tobias (Son of Tobit) and Sarah (Daughter of Raguel); and twice God's blessing is called down. These are things that are important in your marriage as well. This is why getting married in a church says so much more than getting married in a registry office, or just living together without getting married. The wedding in a church says: 'It's as children of God that we come here today to marry; we ask his grace and blessing as we give ourselves to one another today and forever'.

There are two small things in this reading I'd like to explain:

a. *'Tobias said to Raphael: Brother Azarias...': you'll see the reason for the new names if you read the full story. In the story Raphael is an angel in disguise and is using the name Azarias; he brings Tobias off to Raguel to marry Sarah.*
b. *'Brother' and 'sister': at that time these words didn't mean just what we usually understand, children of the same parents. They could also mean people related as cousins, or as husband and wife.*

5. A reading from the book of Tobit (8:4-8)

(After the wedding of Tobias and Sarah, they prayed together like this.)

On the evening of their marriage, Tobias said to Sarah: 'You and I must pray and petition our Lord to win his grace and his protection.' She stood up, and they began praying for protection, and this was how he began:

'You are blessed, O God of our fathers;
blessed too is your name
for ever and ever.
Let the heavens bless you
and all things you have made for evermore.
You it was who created Adam,
you who created Eve his wife
to be his help and support;
and from these two the human race was born.
You it was who said,
'It is not right that the man should be alone;
let us make him a helper like him.'
And so I take my sister
not for any lustful motive, but I do it in singleness of heart.
Be kind enough to have pity on her and on me
and bring us to old age together.'
And together they said, 'Amen, Amen.'

About the reading: Straight talk

Just another small piece from the story of Tobias and Sarah: how they prayed together on their wedding night. If you remember that in the story Sarah had been married seven times before and that her husband died each time on the wedding night, you might understand why Tobias wanted to pray!

Look, too, how they prayed: just speaking to their God in their own words, out loud. For many people nowadays that would take great courage. But if you believe in God and his love for you, why couldn't you? And if you try, you'll find that you'll be sharing a very deep part of your heart and soul with the person you love. As I mentioned earlier, you could use your opportunities for planning the ceremony together as a chance to pray together. Unless you pray together in some way as you come up to the wedding, you're not very likely to pray together on your wedding night – not even if you were in the same situation as Tobias and Sarah! Sunday is a good time to pray together at the church. Another suggestion would be a very short prayer in your own words before and after meals, to ask God to bless you and your food and to give thanks for it. You could take turns at leading it.

So, how about it? Could you decide that, on your wedding night (even if it's well into the morning hours!), you'll take a moment for prayer? On page 230 there's a suggestion for such a moment. Take a look before you rule it out as ridiculous!

6. A reading from the book of Proverbs (31:10-13, 19-20, 30-31)

('Proverbs' are sayings that help to pass on traditional wisdom from one generation to the next. This is from the end of the Book of Proverbs – one person's description of an ideal wife in a time long gone. But how important are the personal qualities this implies?)

The truly capable woman – who can find her?
    She is far beyond the price of pearls.
Her husband's heart has confidence in her,
    from her he will derive no little profit.
Advantage and not hurt she brings him
    all the days of her life.
She selects wool and flax,
    she does her work with eager hands.
She sets her hands to the distaff,
    her fingers grasp the spindle.

She holds out her hands to the poor,
    she opens her arms to the needy.
Charm is deceitful, and beauty empty;
    the woman who fears the Lord is the one to praise.
Give her a share in what her hands have worked for,
    and let her works tell her praises at the city gates.

About the reading: Beyond the price of pearls

Have you ever read Gulliver's Travels *by Dean Jonathan Swift (1667-1745), who was Dean of St Patrick's Cathedral in Dublin? Quick, now: what was Mr Gulliver's first name?*

Swift gave him the first name 'Lemuel', a name from the beginning of this last chapter of the book of Proverbs in the Bible: 'The sayings of Lemuel, king of Massa, taught him by his mother'. Have you some sayings or customs you learned from your parents or others as you were growing up? Are there some sayings or attitudes you would like any children of yours to inherit and value? Proverbs are like that. Not that we follow them slavishly; but they can help us to reflect on matters that face us in our lives today. The reading above is like that. The reading from the book of Sirach on page 122 has some similarities with this reading.

Some people may react strongly, saying that it's a quite out-dated idea of a woman's place. Fair enough. It's not here to say that this is how things should be today. 'She sets her hand to the distaff' – that's a spindle on which wool or flax is wound for spinning: not too many of those in most homes today! If you were to describe a wife, or a husband, who is 'beyond the price of pearls' for the life you'll be living together, how would you do it?

How about a further challenge? This poem from the last chapter of the book of Proverbs, in verses 10 to 31, was written 'alphabetically'. The reading selects just eight verses from it. There are 22 letters in the Hebrew alphabet, whereas there are 26 in the alphabet for the English language. There are 22 verses in this poem, with two lines in each. The first verse begins with the first letter of the Hebrew alphabet, 'Aleph', the next verse with the second letter 'Bet', and so on. Now: would each of you be able to write down 26 (or even 22!) 'verses' of two lines each, about what you appreciate about the other, taking each letter of the alphabet in turn? It needn't be very good poetry, nor rhyme – just let them be from your hearts. If you try this, maybe you'll appreciate how much the writer of the lines in this reading appreciated his wife back then.

If you want to try it using Irish, there are just 18 letters: ABCDEF GHILMN OPRSTU.

7. A reading from the Song of Songs (2:8-10, 14, 16; 8:6-7)

(The Song of Songs is a collection of love songs or poems. This reading tells us of the beauty and strength of love.)

I hear my love.
  See how he comes
  leaping on the mountains,
  bounding over the hills.
My love is like a gazelle,
  like a young stag.
  See where he stands
  behind our wall.
  He looks in at the window,
  he peers through the opening.
My love lifts up his voice,
  he says to me,
  'Come then, my beloved,
  my lovely one, come.
  My dove, hiding in the clefts of the rock,
  in the coverts of the cliff,
  show me your face,
  let me hear your voice;
  for your voice is sweet
  and your face is lovely.'
My love is mine and I am his.

Set me like a seal on your heart,
  like a seal on your arm.
  For love is strong as Death,
  passion as relentless as Sheol.
  The flash of it is a flash of fire,
  a flame of the Lord himself.
Love no flood can quench,
  no torrents drown.

About the reading: Love song

Do you enjoy being in love?

When you find yourself in love with someone, you can begin to understand a lot of love songs that sounded rubbish until now. This book, the Song of Songs, is sometimes called the Song of Solomon, or the Canticle of Canticles. It's really a collection of love songs or poems – no one can be certain how many. There's no story being told: it's just a couple in love being happy with one another and enjoying the thought of one another.

You might think it strange to find all this in the Bible. Why not read it all for yourselves? But remember our first two readings: that God made man and woman to love one another. You can bring it further; often when the Bible speaks of God's love for his people, it talks in terms of a husband and wife. Remember that God really delights in loving us and in being loved by us. He wants us to delight in it too.

The reading hardly needs explanation. It's love poetry. Don't look so much for the ideas in it as for what the person feels who speaks it or sings it.

Just one point of explanation. 'Sheol' is the 'other world' after death. (This was written probably about 500 years before Christ, before ideas on 'Heaven' or 'Hell' had developed.) The meaning is that death and Sheol just cannot be overcome and love is like that too.

It's great when you actually feel like that; but love is not always on a high romantic level: it has to have its feet on the ground. It's a tragedy if love, which is as strong as death, is drowned by bitterness or selfishness or pride. It can overcome these, but this can only be learned the hard way. Knowing that difficulties will come won't prevent them from coming; but it will help you to strengthen you love to overcome them, and so become all the stronger.

8. A reading from the book of Sirach (26:1-4, 13-16)

(Sirach is a wise man, and this book is a collection of wise sayings. This reading tells of the happiness a good wife brings to her husband.)

How blessed is the husband of a really good wife;
    the number of his days will be doubled.
A perfect wife is the joy of her husband,
    he will live out the years of his life in peace.
A good wife is the best of portions,
    reserved for those who fear the Lord;

rich or poor, their hearts will be glad,
their faces cheerful, whatever the season.
The grace of a wife will charm her husband,
her understanding will make him the stronger.
A silent wife is a gift from the Lord,
no price can be put on a well-trained character.
A modest wife is a boon twice over,
a chaste character cannot be over-valued.
Like the sun rising over the mountains of the Lord,
such is the beauty of a good wife in a well-run house.

***About the reading:* Appreciation list**

(This book is also called Ecclesiasticus; it is not included in some Bibles: cf. Note on Tobit, p. 117.)

Take a blank page, and draw a line down the centre. On top of one side write the name of the person you are planning to marry. On top of the other side write your own name.

Compare your lists of good points.

Now comes the hard part. Underneath the other person's name, write down a list of the things you really appreciate about him or her: things done in the past, things that make you happy right now, things that will mean a lot to you in the coming years. Don't rush it – thinking about someone you love a lot is something you can enjoy. Give yourself half an hour, on your own. Just do your best.

Now, an even harder part. Underneath your own name, do the same about yourself. Maybe you'd find it easier to make a list of faults – most people would – but stick to the things you appreciate about yourself: things in the past, in the present and in the future. Take your time over this too – the same time as for the first list. Now, the hardest part: swap papers: swap them with love, a hug and a kiss. You're swapping something very important: what you really appreciate about yourselves. Now read what the other person has written. Read it twice: the first time to get a general picture, the second to understand in your heart what the other is saying about you, and about himself or herself. When you're finished reading, if there's anything you didn't understand, ask. See how much the same or different is the picture you have of yourself, compared with what the other says. You may learn something about yourself.

The lists won't be the same as in this reading (nor the same as Psalm 112 below, about the man) of course; but if the Bible in this reading shows appreciation of a really good wife, it's good for you to do the same for each other. Quite often we forget to do this: we just see the faults and only show appreciation much too late. You'll be growing and developing as husband and wife in your marriage. You could try doing this again after you're married a year or two; or how about every year as an anniversary present?

9: A reading from the book of Jeremiah (31:31-34)

(Jeremiah tells us that God wants to put love deep in our hearts – he will really be our God, and we will be his people. At this wedding, bride and groom also give one another their deepest love; they will really belong to one another.)

Look, the days are coming, the Lord declares, when I shall make a new covenant with the House of Israel (and the House of Judah), but not like the covenant I made with their ancestors the day I took them by the hand to bring them out of Egypt, a covenant which they broke, even though I was their Master, the Lord declares. No, this is the covenant I shall make with the House of Israel when those days have come, the Lord declares. Within them I shall plant my Law, writing it on their hearts. Then I shall be their God and they will be my people. There will be no further need for everyone to teach neighbour or brother, saying, 'Learn to know the Lord!' No, they will all know me, from the least to the greatest, the Lord declares.

About the reading: An agreeable agreement

When you decided to marry, you made a promise to each other. It's not something you bargained over, tit for tat, it's an agreement made out of love; an agreement looking forward to something deeper and more permanent: you were looking forward to the time when you'd 'write it on your hearts'.

It was like that between God and his people. Their agreement or 'covenant' was at Mount Sinai, at the time of Moses. The Covenant was that this God, whom they knew as 'the Lord' or 'Yahweh' was to be their god, and they were to be his people. (At that time, they thought that each people or nation or place had its own god, who was not a god for other peoples and places.) You may remember reading, or seeing a film, about Moses receiving what we call 'The Ten Commandments' on the mountain, with these terms of the Covenant written in stone. The people were looking forward to their 'New Covenant' that Jeremiah talks about in this reading. In this New Covenant, God's law of love wouldn't be written on stone or paper, but on their hearts.

And in the same way, you can say to each other: 'On our wedding day, deep within you I will plant my love, writing on your heart. Then I will be yours and you shall be mine'.

It will be a love that will grow and develop and change all through the years of your life together. Isn't that why you plant something? And there won't be any need for you to wonder whether you love each other: you'll know it from your life together.

The New Covenant came with Jesus. He wants each of us to know that he loves us all, and he want us to know it as surely as you know you love each other in your marriage. Your marrying as Christians means a lot to you; to the rest of the world, it says: 'Look! we love each other completely and forever. That's how Jesus loves us too and that's how he loves you as well'.

You really can know for yourselves that that is true. All you've got to do is to take him at his word. That's what you'll be doing as husband and wife every time you celebrate Mass – you celebrate his love in you.

Responsorial Psalms

When a person speaks to us, we normally respond. That's what the 'Responsorial Psalm' is for.

When a person says something of particular importance to us, we might take a few moments to think about it before we respond. Having heard the first reading, it can be good to take a few moments before we respond. If this seems good, why not ask for a short silence (even just fifteen seconds or so) before continuing with the Psalm? Sometimes people are afraid of silences, in case others think we've forgotten what to do next! The person who takes the first reading, or the person leading the Psalm, could say something like: 'We take a few moments to let that sink in'.

The Psalms are prayers in song from the Bible. They are not 'readings' to be read, but prayers to be prayed. Ideally, the Responsorial Psalm would be sung, with a refrain or response for people to sing after each few lines. St Augustine said many centuries ago: 'Singing is praying twice'.

If you have one or more people to lead in the singing at your wedding, ask about having a 'cantor' – a person to lead the singing of the Psalm. Two or three can act together as cantor. Or perhaps one or more of the guests could prepare and lead this. (They don't have to be professional performers.) There are many such arrangements for Psalms. The singing could be done as follows:

1. *If there is an organ or musical instrument, the melody of the Response is played first. (It could also be rehearsed while people are gathering.)*
2. *The cantor(s) sings the Response while all listen.*
3. *All respond by singing the Response.*
4. *The cantor(s) sings the first section of the Psalm (or, if not sung, a person leads all in prayer with the first section spoken).*
5. *All join in singing the Response, led by the cantor(s); and so forth, after each section of the Psalm.*

If your wedding is taking place during the Easter season, you may like to choose a sung arrangement of 'Alleluia!', usually repeated a few times, for all to sing as the Response. Alleluia simply means 'Praise God!'

There may be Psalms which those present may know, and could sing together.

If the Psalm is being spoken rather than sung, the person leading it announces the response at the beginning. Then, after each section, those present need to know when to come in with the Response. This is best done by the person speaking the verses of the Psalm, perhaps like this: at the end of each section, the person speaking the verses slows down a little and changes tone of voice, and then looks up at the congregation with a short pause; and then leads in the repetition of the Response. This signals the congregation to join in the Response. Where the text of the Psalm in the book indicates the Response, this is like a stage direction for the person leading: the word 'Response' should NOT be announced each time.

1. Psalm 32

(Psalm 32 is about God's goodness to his people.)
The response is:
The Lord fills the earth with his love!

(i) They are happy, whose God is the Lord,
the people he has chosen as his own.
The Lord looks on those who revere him,
on those who hope in his love. – *Response*

(ii) Our soul is waiting for the Lord.
The Lord is our help and our shield.
In him do our hearts find joy.
We trust in his holy name. – *Response*

(iii) May your love be upon us, O Lord,
as we place all our hope in you. – *Response*

2. Psalm 33

(Psalm 33 is a general song of confidence in God's goodness.)
The response is either:
I will bless the Lord at all times.
or: Taste and see that the Lord is good.

(i) I will bless the Lord at all times,
his praise always on my lips;
in the Lord my soul shall make its boast.
The humble shall hear and be glad. – *Response*

(ii) Glorify the Lord with me.
Together let us praise his name.
I sought the Lord and he answered me;
from all my terrors he set me free. – *Response*

(iii) Look towards him and be radiant;
Let your faces not be abashed.
This poor man called; the Lord heard him
and rescued him from all his distress. – *Response*

(iv) The angel of the Lord is encamped
around those who revere him, to rescue them.
Taste and see that the Lord is good.
He is happy who seeks refuge in him. – *Response*

3. Psalm 102

(Psalm 102 says that God's love is like a father's love, and will never end.) 'Fear' is mentioned in this psalm, and in the following two psalms. What on earth is fear doing at a wedding celebration? Most people experience fear at some times in their life. It can play an important part in getting us to respond to danger! Here, however, we look at another side of it. With a person who loves you very much, more than you could ever deserve, there can at times be a feeling of such wonder and mystery and awe that you may have a sense of hardly being worthy to be part of that person's world. It can seem even almost

a fear – not in the 'awful' sense, but in the 'awesome' sense! It's this 'awesome' feeling we're talking about here. You may at times feel this kind of 'fear' as you come close to your wedding day. If you can feel this with another human being, what would it be like if you were to begin to have a sense of the God of all creation, who wants you to know 'I have loved you with an everlasting love'?

Either of two responses: The Lord is compassion and love.
or: The love of the Lord is everlasting upon those who hold him in fear.

(i) My soul, give thanks to the Lord,
all my being, bless his holy name.
My soul, give thanks to the Lord
and never forget all his blessings. – *Response*

(ii) The Lord is compassion and love,
slow to anger and rich in mercy.
As a father has compassion on his sons,
the Lord has pity on those who fear him. – *Response*

(iii) The love of the Lord is everlasting
upon those who hold him in fear;
his justice reaches out to their children's children
when they keep his covenant in truth. – *Response*

4. Psalm 111

(Psalm 111 is about the kind of person who lives the way God wants us to: the kind of person who is like a light in the darkness.)

The response is either: Happy the man who takes delight in the Lord's commands. *or:* Alleluia.

(i) Happy the man who fears the Lord,
who takes delight in his commands;
his sons will be powerful on earth;
the children of the upright are blessed. – *Response*

(ii) Riches and wealth are in his house;
his justice stands firm for ever.
He is a light in the darkness for the upright;
he is generous, merciful and just. – *Response*

(iii) The good man takes pity and lends,
he conducts his affairs with honour.
The just man will never waver:
he will be remembered for ever. – *Response*

(iv) He has no fear of evil news;
with a firm heart he trusts in the Lord.
With a steadfast heart he will not fear;
he will see the downfall of his foes. – *Response*

(v) Open-handed, he gives to the poor;
his justice stands firm for ever.
His head will be raised in glory. – *Response*

5. Psalm 127

(Psalm 127 is a song of the blessings of living God's ways: one of these blessings is a prosperous home! The blessing from Zion (Jerusalem) is a blessing from the central city for God's people, just as, nowadays, we have a custom of sending for a Papal Blessing from Rome. On fear, see the introduction to Psalm 102, above.)

The response is either: Blessed are those who fear the Lord.
or: Indeed thus shall be blessed the man who fears the Lord.

(i) O blessed are those who fear the Lord
and walk in his ways!
By the labour of your hands you shall eat.
You will be happy and prosper. – *Response*

(ii) Your wife shall be like a fruitful vine
in the heart of your house;

your children like shoots of the olive,
around your table. – *Response*

(iii) Indeed thus shall be blessed
the man who fears the Lord.
May the Lord bless you from Zion
All the days of your life! – *Response*

6. Psalm 144

(Psalm 144 praises God for his goodness – the kind of goodness we need too!)
The response is: How good is the Lord to all!

(i) The Lord is kind and full of compassion,
slow to anger, abounding in love.
How good is the Lord to all,
compassionate to all his creatures. – *Response*

(ii) All your creatures shall thank you, O Lord,
and your friends shall repeat their blessing.
The eyes of all creatures look to you
and you give them their food in due time. – *Response*

(iii) The Lord is just in all his ways
and loving in all his deeds.
He is close to all who call him,
who call on him from their hearts. – *Response*

7. Psalm 148

(Psalm 148 sees the splendour of creation as a hymn in praise of God. This day in your life is also a hymn of praise to God with the rest of the world.)
The response is either: Praise the name of the Lord.
or: Alleluia.

(i) Praise the Lord from the heavens,
praise him in the heights.

Praise him, all his angels,
praise him, all his host! – *Response*

(ii) Praise him, sun and moon;
praise him, shining stars.
Praise him, highest heavens
and the waters above the heavens. – *Response*

(iii) All mountains and hills,
and fruit trees and cedars,
beasts, wild and tame,
reptiles and birds on the wing. – *Response*

(iv) All earth's kings and peoples,
earth's princes and rulers:
young men and maidens,
old men together with children. – *Response*

(v) Let them praise the name of the Lord,
for he alone is exalted.
The splendour of his name
reaches beyond heaven and earth. – *Response*

New Testament Readings

These readings tell us some of the things the first Christians learned from knowing Jesus Christ – what they learned especially about life and love. There are four Gospels in the New Testament, together with a collection of other writings, mostly letters. These readings are taken from those other writings. Read them, and see what any of them can mean for your wedding.

At the end of the reading the reader says, 'This is the Word of the Lord', and all respond, 'Thanks be to God'.

1. A reading from the letter of St Paul to the Romans (8:31-35, 37-39)
(This tells us of the strength of God's love as we see it in Jesus Christ. It's a love we all want to live and make our own.)

If God is for us, who can be against us? Since he did not spare his own Son, but gave him up for the sake of all of us, then can we not expect that with him he will freely give us all his gifts?

Who can bring any accusation against those that God has chosen? When God grants saving justice, who can condemn? Are we not sure that it is Christ Jesus, who died – yes and more, who was raised from the dead and is at God's right hand – and who is adding his plea for us? Can anything cut us off from the love of Christ – can hardships or distress, or persecution, or lack of food and clothing, or threats or violence? No; we come through all these things triumphantly victorious, by the power of him who loved us.

For I am certain of this: neither death nor life, nor angels, nor principalities, nothing already in existence and nothing still to come, nor any power, nor the heights nor the depths, nor any created thing whatever, will be able to come between us and the love of God, known to us in Christ Jesus our Lord.

About the reading: Odds-on-favourite

Have you ever felt that the odds are all against you? That life is an uphill struggle all the way, and that you'll be lucky to scrape through at all? From now on you have each other. You can support each other in difficulty, and depression and sorrow. You've got a friend you can really rely on; who'll stick by you for better or worse, for richer or poorer, in sickness and in health; only death will separate you.

You've got another friend, too: God. He's on your side. So the odds aren't against you – they're very much in your favour. He isn't one to condemn you – after all, he sent his son, Jesus, to live and die and rise again for us. Not even death itself will separate us from the love God has shown us in Jesus.

Love doesn't get rid of all difficulties – if it did, Paul would not have had any need to write this. Our faith in God does not mean there is no evil or pain or death. Our faith means that we can look straight in the face of the very worst darkness, and still put our hand in the hand of God – as Jesus did on the cross. Your faith in each other says that your love will see you through each and every difficulty, even ones that seem to have no answer. Maybe you could think of your love as a 'reflection' – an image of God's love, made real here and now between you. That's one of the things it means when we say that marriage is a sacrament: your unconditional love for one another makes God's love for us present to us, both on your wedding day and all your married life.

Take those last few lines of this reading, beginning with 'I am certain of this...': there is a challenge for all Christians here. This is the love we believe God has given us in Jesus Christ. We Christians are called to be the living presence of Jesus Christ in our world today. If this is so, then we want to be able to say those lines, finishing with 'will be able to come between us and the love of God, known to us in all of us Christians, the Church'. And we want to be able to look at your Christian marriage, and say those lines, finishing with 'made known to us in you!'

Could you get together now and decide on having something definite in your home that will remind you of the love we see in Jesus Christ? For instance, a picture, or a statue, or a poster, or crucifix, or something that you both like, and that will have this meaning. If you do this not just as a matter of form, but deliberately, because you want to, it will always inspire you.

2. A reading from the letter of St Paul to the Romans (12:1-2, 9-18)
(St Paul tells us to be practical. Love can't be just in the mind – it must show in our bodies, in what we do. But neither can it be just an act – it must be sincere.)

(Short version: omit text between brackets.)
I urge you, brothers, remembering the mercies of God, to offer your bodies as a living sacrifice, dedicated and acceptable to God; that is the kind of worship for you, as sensible people.

Do not model your behaviour on the contemporary world, but let the renewing of your minds transform you, so that you may discern for yourselves what is the will of God – what is good and acceptable and mature.

Let love be without any pretence. Avoid what is evil; stick to what is good. In brotherly love let your feelings of deep affection for one another come to expression, and regard others as more important than yourself. In the service of the Lord, work not half-heartedly but with conscientiousness and an eager spirit.

Be joyful in hope, persevere in hardship; keep praying regularly;

share with any of God's holy people who are in need; look for opportunities to be hospitable.

[Bless your persecutors; never curse them, bless them.
Rejoice with others when they rejoice, and be sad with those in sorrow.
Give the same consideration to all others alike. Pay no regard to social standing, but meet humble people on their own terms. Do not congratulate yourself on your own wisdom.
Never pay back evil with evil, but bear in mind the ideals that all regard with respect.
As much as possible, and to the utmost of your ability, be at peace with everyone.]

About the reading: A new programme

Writing a letter is hard work. Writing to someone you don't know is even harder, because you don't know what the person you're writing to is going to think, even if you're trying to say something very important. And getting a letter like that from someone you don't know, you might think: 'What right has that person to tell me how to live?'

Paul was writing to people in Rome that he didn't know, and he gives just general advice to the Christians there. You could apply every sentence of this reading to yourself, especially coming up to your wedding.

For example: 'Let your behaviour change, modelled by your new mind'. He was talking to people who were becoming Christians; but you're starting a new way of life now, too: you need to have a 'new mind' and changed behaviour. From now on your wife or husband is THE person in your life.

The things Paul mentions could inspire you for a long time: sincerity, respect, untiring effort, earnestness, hope, prayer, hospitality, blessing your enemies, sharing your joy and sorrow, kindness, no revenge, peace. These would make a programme for a lifetime! You could even use these for examining your conscience; measure yourself as a friend, and as husband and wife, against these items.

3. A reading from the letter of St Paul to the Romans (15:1b-3a, 5-7, 13)

(Coming towards the end of this letter, St Paul encourages us to be people known for their unselfishness and for being a people of hope, since we are disciples of Jesus Christ.)

It is for us not to please ourselves. Each of us must consider his neighbour's good, so that we support one another. Christ did not indulge his own feelings, either.

Now the God of perseverance and encouragement give you all the same purpose, following the example of Christ Jesus, so that you may together give glory to the God and Father of our Lord Jesus Christ with one heart. Accept one another, then, for the sake of God's glory, as Christ accepted you.

May the God of hope fill you with all joy and peace in your faith, so that in the power of the Holy Spirit you may be rich in hope.

***About the reading:* What a hope!**

'I hope it doesn't rain on our wedding day!' Sometimes when we use the word 'hope', it seems to mean: 'I'd very much like things to turn out well, but I don't really think they will!' To hope for something implies that we don't already have it, of course, but at times it's more the 'forlorn hope' we think of, rather than the 'looking forward to'. It's understandable, when it involves factors beyond our control, like the weather. It's different when we're speaking of someone whose love we trust in. This is what St Paul is speaking of in that last sentence. The God Paul knows is a God of love and life and compassion: this is where Paul's hope lies. This is where your 'hope' in one another comes from too. Coming to your wedding day, there's a sureness about your hopes for the future, because they have a sure foundation: you have an unconditional promise from the person you marry, and you yourself give a similar unconditional promise. You know you have your failings and limitations, but you can decide that you're going to live, not to please yourself, but to bring life and love to someone else. You can't know for sure what your life will be like next week or next year or in twenty years' time, but you CAN say: 'This is my decision, and I will be faithful'. Look again at the last sentence of the reading. Could there be any more hope-full day than your wedding day?

4. A reading from the first letter of St Paul to the Corinthians (6:13-15, 17-20)

(St Paul says that our bodies themselves are holy. This has special meaning for married people: it makes marriage all the more important.)

The body is not for sexual immorality; it is for the Lord, and the Lord is for the body. God raised up the Lord and he will raise us up too by his power.

Do you not realise that your bodies are members of Christ's body? Anyone who attaches himself to the Lord is one spirit with him.

Keep away from sexual immorality. All other sins that people may commit are done outside the body; but the sexually immoral person sins against his own body. Do you not realise that your body is the temple of the Holy Spirit, who is in you and whom you received from God?

You are not your own property, then; you have been bought at a price. So use your body for the glory of God.

About the reading: Love in control

Home is a place we can relax in; a place where we can be ourselves. We don't have to pretend – we're with people who love us. But that doesn't mean we can do just whatever we like. Love gives us tremendous freedom in what we say and do, but that doesn't mean 'Anything goes!' Love is 'free' in that it can never be bought or sold or earned, but it's quite clear that there are many things which are a contradiction of real love. St Paul was very keen on the idea that becoming a Christian gives us a great freedom – a freedom to live and love in a new way; a freedom from being a slave to the many things that contradict true love. We have the freedom to eat our food; but we are not doomed to eat that chocolate! There were people in Paul's time who seemed to think that sexual intercourse is as inevitable as taking food, and to be satisfied as freely. Does that sound familiar? Much of today's culture seems to see it as only natural and inevitable that when two people find a sexual attraction between them, this leads almost immediately to sexual intercourse, whether in bed or anywhere else. Paul puts quite a different approach.

This is a very important subject for an engaged couple to discuss seriously. It's something that affects you deeply, both before marriage, and in the years following. It can happen, even for a couple in a very good engagement or marriage, that one of them may meet another person and find a sexual attraction, perhaps very intense. It's part of the way we are as human beings. How would you handle such a situation? It's important to keep in mind that it's just PART of what we are. Of course, it could be exciting, but no matter how intense it may be, we are not doomed to be sucked in by it. It does not mean you would be a bad wife or husband if you come across this. What is important is what you do about it. There are practical steps you take to make sure it does not take over your life or destroy your marriage. This is where real freedom comes in.

Be clear on the larger picture. Your real life and freedom are with the person you married on your wedding day. Since you are part of one another now, this is your life. Remember the line from the book of Genesis on page 113 about leaving father and mother, and becoming one body. The last thing you would want to do is to sin against your own body.

Amazingly, St Paul sees our relationship with Jesus Christ like that too. 'Your bodies are members of Christ's body!' Does this seem very strange? Your love for one another in marriage as Christians not only unites you very closely and intimately with one another; it also unites you closely and intimately with Jesus Christ so that, together, you can bring his life and love to the world today. You want love to be the inspiration of your life together. You also know that love is not always easy. However perfect and complete your love may be on your wedding day, there are still many other stages to come in the growth of your love. This is how the glory of God will be seen in your life together.

5. A reading from the first letter of St Paul to the Corinthians (12:31-13:8)

(In this reading, St Paul gives us a hymn in praise of love – the kind of love you would like yours to be!)

Set your mind on the higher gifts. And now I am going to put before you the best way of all.

Though I command languages both human and angelic, if I speak without love, I am no more than a gong booming or a cymbal clashing. And though I have the power of prophecy, to penetrate all mysteries and knowledge, and though I have all the faith necessary to move mountains, if I am without love, I am nothing. Though I should give away to the poor all that I possess, and even give up my body to be burned, if I am without love, it will do me no good whatever.

Love is always patient and kind; love is never jealous;
love is not boastful or conceited, it is never rude and never seeks its own advantage,
it does not take offence or store up grievances.
Love does not rejoice at wrongdoing, but finds its joy in the truth.
It is always ready to make allowances, to trust, to hope and to endure whatever comes.
Love never comes to an end.

About the reading: The reason for it all

Could you imagine yourselves arranging your wedding and all that it involves, if you didn't love each other? You might have the most beautiful wedding of the year, with the biggest crowd and the best music and photographs in colour in all the newspapers and magazines; and if it weren't for love, it would just be a big empty splash: a gong booming for nothing.

You might get the most wonderful wedding presents. You might know all there is to know about marriage, both in theory and in practice. You might know how to overcome mountains of difficulties and believe in yourselves completely; but without love, you're nothing at all.

You might do all the right things, so that everybody would say that you're wonderful. You might be famous for your generosity, and make enormous sacrifices, but it will do no good at all without love.

I'm not talking about a romantic love, which is great as long as you feel good. Neither is Paul. It's down-to-earth love. Read through the reading now. When you finish it, go back to the part that begins: 'Love is always patient and kind', and read it again as far as 'and to endure whatever comes'. You should have got the meaning pretty well now.

When you've done that, now try this: read over that part of the reading again, and this time everywhere you see the word love, put in yourself: 'I am always patient...' That will give you something to aim for! There are difficulties that come from within ourselves: impatience, unkindness, jealousy, boasting, conceit, rudeness and selfishness. There are difficulties that are sparked off by another person: taking offence, having grudges, being pleased (even just secretly) when things go wrong for another person, not being happy at another person doing well. And there are difficulties that come from life – we might say from God: not really leaving ourselves in his hands and trusting his strength to make us strong no matter what happens. All these difficulties can wear us down and break us, but they can never break love. Love simply does not come to an end.

6. A reading from the letter of St Paul to the Ephesians (4:1-6)

(In just these five sentences, written from prison, Paul has a short programme for lifelong marriages – and for all Christians.)

I, the prisoner in the Lord, urge you therefore to lead a life worthy of the vocation to which you were called.

With all humility and gentleness, and with patience, support each other in love. Take every care to preserve the unity of the Spirit by the peace that binds you together.

There is one Body, one Spirit, just as one hope is the goal of your calling by God. There is one Lord, one faith, one baptism, and one God and Father of all, over all, through all and within all.

About the reading: The power of one!

European Union, Trade Union, Credit Union, United States, United Kingdom, Manchester United… how many 'unions' or 'uniteds' are part of your life? How important are they? Then we have the opposite. The Irish writer, Brendan Behan, is reported to have said that the first item on the agenda of any new organisation is 'The Split' – when people come together to tackle issues, they find there are matters they cannot agree on, and so they split into two or more groups. Has that been part of your life too?

People working together can accomplish so much. Think of how a sports team can work together, or the people responsible for air travel, or the people who had a part in bringing out this book! It doesn't mean all those people are clones with the same personalities and opinions. The varieties you get in people make them so much more interesting, and their 'union' so much more enriching. One of the great challenges for Christians is to find how, with all their differences, to be one with one another. And one of the challenges for two people who marry is to be one. It's one of the really beautiful experiences, to know people who, with all the ways they are different, are in some way really united.

Paul, in this reading, says: 'Take every care to preserve the unity of the Spirit by the peace that binds you together'. Then he uses the word 'one' seven times to bring home the faith sources of our unity as Christians. As two people united in love and marriage, you want to 'preserve the unity' of your union by the peace that binds you together. What are the sources of your union? Could you list some of the things that are the foundation of your union, just as Paul did for our faith-communion? What you list may not be at all the kind of things that Paul lists – that's okay. But maybe you could think about this: if you belong to the same Christian Church or communion, have you been able to share something of your faith with one another? Sometimes people feel it's so private and personal that they would find it difficult to do this. But if you can, you may find that it gives you an extra level of unity that you never expected! You don't have to be completely alike in all you believe – otherwise you'd never learn from one another. There are some suggestions in the section 'Could We Work On It?' on page 45. The sources of unity that Paul lists can be a source of unity and strength for you too.

And if you do not belong to the same Christian Church or communion? If you have strongly held beliefs which differ? No reason to avoid it or fight about it – you can still be 'united'. It's not your fault that the Churches and faiths are divided. Your unity can be an example that, please God, people of every faith can be inspired by! There is a saying attributed to St Augustine more than 1500 years ago: 'In what is necessary, let there be unity. In what is doubtful, let there be liberty. In all things, let there be charity'. Charity here is another word for love.

7. A reading from the letter of St Paul to the Ephesians (5:2, 21-33)

(St Paul was writing to Christians at Ephesus in his day, and here in this passage he gave husbands and wives an ideal to work for: the kind of love and respect there is between Christ and his Church.)

(Short version: omit text between brackets.)

Follow Christ by loving as he loved you, giving himself up for us as an offering and a sweet-smelling sacrifice to God.

[Be subject to one another out of reverence for Christ.

Wives should be subject to their husbands as to the Lord, since, as Christ is head of the Church and saves the whole body, so is a husband the head of his wife; and as the Church is subject to Christ, so should wives be to their husbands, in everything.]

Husbands should love their wives, just as Christ loved the Church and sacrificed himself for her to make her holy by washing her in cleansing water with a form of words, so that when he took the Church to himself she would be glorious, with no speck or wrinkle or anything like that, but holy and faultless.

In the same way, husbands must love their wives as they love their own bodies; for a man to love his wife is for him to love himself. A man never hates his own body, but he feeds it and looks after it; and that is the way Christ treats the Church, because we are parts of his Body.

This is why a man leaves his father and mother and becomes attached to his wife, and the two become one flesh.

This mystery has great significance, but I am applying it to Christ and the Church.

[To sum up: you also, each one of you, must love his wife as he loves himself; and let every wife respect her husband.]

About the reading: Mystery story

There's no shortage of love stories on television, in magazines, comics, films, and so on. Are there any of them that you'd model your marriage on? In this reading, St Paul very definitely gives us the one to follow: Jesus Christ.

Just keep in mind that this was written nearly 2000 years ago, and the accepted place of husband and wife at that time and place was not at all what we would envisage nowadays! (You'll find the same in the reading from the first letter of St Peter on page 146.) We can learn from that. So when you read what Paul says, maybe you could ask yourselves: 'What kind of person is Jesus Christ? How could Jesus Christ bring extra wisdom and inspiration into our marriage today?'

The first sentence is the most important one. All the rest is Paul's way of applying that sentence to husbands and wives – and he's equally demanding on both. The standard of love and subjection and self-giving he sets are what Jesus did. For Jesus, the way to be great is to be a servant to everybody, and to love one another as he loves us, his people, his Church.

Paul uses a sentence from the book of Genesis (second Old Testament reading, page 113): 'A man must leave father and mother and be joined to his wife and the two will become one body'. And he says there's more meaning in that than we ever suspected: in fact, he says, it applies to Christ and the Church – that they too are joined together as one body. From this early time in the life of Christians, they made a connection between the love uniting husband and wife, and the love uniting Jesus Christ and his people, the Church.

So when you live your lives together in love as Christians, you're a living example of Christ's love. You know how good it is to visit a really loving home. It's a blessing of God you experience. May your visitors experience the same in your home.

8. A reading from the letter of St Paul to the Philippians (4:4-9)

(St Paul here is very up-beat, wanting us to keep in mind that, even when life brings trouble and sadness, that's never the full picture. Learn to focus on what's going for us!)

Always be joyful in the Lord; I repeat, be joyful.

Let your good sense be obvious to everybody. The Lord is near.

Never worry about anything; but tell God all your desires of every kind in prayer and petition shot through with gratitude, and the peace of God which is beyond our understanding will guard your hearts and your thoughts in Christ Jesus.

Finally, let your minds be filled with everything that is true, everything that is honourable, everything that is upright and pure, everything that we love and admire, with whatever is good and praiseworthy. Keep doing everything you learnt from me and were told by me and have heard or seen me doing. Then the God of peace will be with you.

About the reading: Getting a mindful

Does this make sense to you at all? How can you tell a person to be joyful? How can you tell someone never to worry about anything? With all that's coming at us all the time, how could we be sure to fill our minds with everything we love and admire?

If joy is something that depends on what comes to us from outside, clearly there's not much we can do to 'be joyful'. But if it's something that comes from deep inside, the kind of person you are and how you see the world, then there's a lot we can do. It's what might be called nowadays 'cognitive therapy': learning a way to perceive the world around us, and ourselves too. Maybe Paul is far ahead of his time!

Normally, it is possible for us to direct our minds. In any relationship, we can choose to take notice of the needs of another person or of many people, even when we have worries of our own. We don't deny that there are other matters, but we choose to attend to what is of greater importance. In preparing for a wedding, and in married life afterwards, there can be many things, even many things that are good in themselves, which can begin almost to take over a person's life. Here is where it is important to focus on what comes first. To focus on what is urgent may be desirable; but if it prevents a person attending to what is really important in the overall scheme, it can be very damaging. A squabble about a smaller matter may destroy the performance of a whole team. So it's good to practise taking time to agree on the priorities. Coming up to a wedding may be an opportunity to practise!

Believe it or not, it is possible to be joyful even when the world is falling apart. But only if there's a foundation deeper than any of the other things that affect us. If I'm joyful in myself, or because of you, that's good. Paul's phrase is to be 'joyful in the Lord!' If there ever was a time for this, could it be on your wedding day? Then your joy in one another will be all the deeper.

9. A reading from the letter of St Paul to the Colossians (3:12-17)
(He suggests some ways in which the message of Christ can find a home with you!)

As the chosen of God, then, the holy people whom he loves, you are to be clothed in heartfelt compassion, in generosity and humility, gentleness and patience. Bear with one another; forgive each other if one of you has a complaint against another. The Lord has forgiven you; now you must do the same. Over all these clothes, put on love, the perfect bond.

And may the peace of Christ reign in your hearts, because it is for this that you were called together in one body. Always be thankful.

Let the Word of Christ, in all its richness, find a home with you. Teach each other, and advise each other, in all wisdom. With gratitude in your hearts sing psalms and hymns and inspired songs to God; and whatever you say or do, let it be in the name of the Lord Jesus, in thanksgiving to God the Father through him.

***About the reading:* Ladies' and gents' outfitter!**
You get out of bed. Sometimes, maybe, it's a pleasure to get up and get ready for a new day. Other times it's not a pleasure, if you're dog-tired or worried or sick. You wash and put on your clothes, and go out to fact the world. Is there anything else you should put on? St Paul gives a few suggestions about what to clothe yourself with. It's not a matter of: 'Start the day with a smile, and get it over with'. Look what Paul puts first: the good news. Count your blessings – even just one or two, and then the 'clothes' will follow. You are God's chosen race, his saints – he loves you! Not: 'If you do this and this and... then you'll be God's people', but: 'You are.' Could you build a thought like that into each morning as you get up?

Then some people are in bad form in the morning. There's a fight – what then? 'Bear with one another; forgive each other as soon as the quarrel begins.' Difficult? Yes. Impossible? No. If there is love to hold all the other clothes together. You're one body; let the peace of Christ have the final say. He has forgiven you.

Has Christ's message a home with you? Will it have, when you're married? If it isn't home with you yet, you could use the Bible readings in this book to open the door. 'Teach each other, advise each other.' – 'What? Is that to be a part of your marriage?' Is there so much pride there that you can't say: 'Actually, I think you're right there', or 'I'm sorry, I made a mistake', or 'Thanks for telling me that'? If you've something to be thankful for together (and haven't you each other?) could you say thanks to God together? Or even sing it? You're Christians living the new life Christ has given you; let everything you do be what he would want you to do. That way, your very life will be your 'thanks' to God the Father.

10. A reading from the letter to the Hebrews (13:1-4a, 5-6a)

(This is called a letter, but it is more like a homily, a talk to encourage and guide Christians. The reading is from some closing remarks. Where it says to 'love each other like brothers', the word 'brothers' in the usage of the time included sisters too – all the family of believers.)

Continue to love each other like brothers, and remember always to welcome strangers, for by doing this, some people have entertained angels without knowing it. Keep in mind those who are in prison, as though you were in prison with them; and those who are being badly treated, since you too are in the body. Marriage must be honoured by all, and marriages must be kept undefiled. Put avarice out of your lives and be content with whatever you have; God himself has said: 'I shall not fail you or desert you'; and so we can say with confidence: With the Lord on my side, I fear nothing.

***About the reading:* Looking outwards**

Celebrating your wedding is a beginning: the beginning of a lifelong mission. Your mission is not to spend the rest of your lives just looking at one another in a private cosy huddle – even if it's a holy private cosy huddle! The gift of love that you experience from one another is a gift that can inspire other people outside your marriage and family. The words of encouragement in the reading were not written just for married Christians, but for all believers.

The writer says that the love you live can be one that welcomes strangers. The bit about entertaining angels refers to a story of Abraham and Sarah (husband and wife) in chapter 18 of the book of Genesis at the beginning of the Bible. Keeping in mind those in prison and badly treated could refer to Christians facing persecution; but it can apply equally to those in prison for crimes. 'Since you too are in the body' can remind us that we are members of the one Body of Christ, which we call the Church.

'Marriage must be honoured' is frequently not the case, both in the media and in everyday experience: the 'defiling' of marriage can make a more dramatic story-line

for a film or book. By honouring your own marriage, you can also encourage others to do the same.

'Avarice' is greed: 'I want... I want...' There can be a lot of pressure on a married couple in providing a home and the necessities of life, and we can be seduced at times by the pressure of life around us to be greedy for more and bigger and better and more up-to-date. You may find yourselves at times faced with a decision to choose less of what you can have or buy or earn, in order to safeguard and develop what is of far greater value: your marriage and your family.

Wouldn't it be great on your wedding day to be able to say those last three lines of the reading from your heart, knowing the truth of them?

11. A reading from the first letter of Peter (3:1-9)

(St Peter, who was married himself, says in this reading that husbands and wives should have great consideration for one another; they should always work for harmony.)

Wives should be obedient to your husbands. Then if there are some husbands who do not believe the Word, they may find themselves won over, without a word spoken, by the way their wives behave, when they see the reverence and purity of your way of life.

Your adornment should be not an exterior one, consisting of braided hair or gold jewellery or fine clothing, but the interior disposition of the heart, consisting in the imperishable quality of a gentle and peaceful spirit, so precious in the sight of God. That was how the holy women of the past dressed themselves attractively, they hoped in God and were submissive to their husbands; like Sarah, who was obedient to Abraham, and called him her lord. You are now her children, as long as you live good lives free from fear and worry.

In the same way, husbands must always treat their wives with consideration in their life together, respecting a woman as one who, though she may be the weaker partner, is equally an heir to the generous gift of life. This will prevent anything from coming in the way of your prayers.

Finally: you should all agree among yourselves and be sympathetic; love the brothers, have compassion and be self-effacing.

Never repay one wrong with another, or one abusive word with another; instead, repay with a blessing. That is what you are called to do, so that you inherit a blessing.

About the reading: Speaking from (Peter's) experience

Think of some happily married couples you know – maybe each of you could write down the names of three or four such couples. Now think about how those people work things out together in their marriage. First write down the things about them that you'd like to see in your own marriage. Then write down the things that you think you could work out in a better way yourselves in your marriage. No one marriage will be exactly the same as any other.

Then read this piece from St Peter's letter, and ask yourselves what you can learn from him. (St Peter was married!) As in the reading from the letter to the Ephesians on page 141, just keep in mind that this was written nearly 2000 years ago, and the accepted place of husband and wife at that time and place was not at all what we would envisage nowadays. We use our common sense, and apply it to our situation today. Here are some of the things the letter says, which you may find worth thinking about.

He tells wives to be obedient – but look at the reason: so as to help their husbands to come to the Lord. 'Obey' doesn't mean 'Be a doormat'! There are three different kinds of obedience; it's clear enough which to aim for:

1. *Obedience of the slave: obey because you have to, or because you're afraid.*
2. *Obedience of the mercenary: for what you can get out of it for yourself.*
3. *Obedience of the lover: out of love for the other person, you want to please, and you want to accept the love the other is offering.*

'Your adornment should not be an exterior one.' He makes it quite clear that what a person is like inside is more important than how beautiful or handsome or well dressed or made-up.

'In the same way, husbands…'. The first four words are important. Whatever the natural differences between how men and women are made, the most important thing is that husband and wife are equal as children of God. Then comes an interesting point: 'This will prevent anything from coming in the way of your prayers'. If you're happy in how you live your love together, you'll find great happiness in your relationships with God. If there's something you're not happy about between yourselves, you'll find you're not at ease with God; and if there's something coming between you and God, you'll probably notice some strain in your relationship with one another. As St John says (in reading 13): 'God is love'.

Peter's five virtues are worth making your own; the importance of agreeing with one another; of being sympathetic; of loving 'the brothers', and not just one or two people; of having compassion for people in trouble; and of not insisting on your rights, but being self-effacing. What he says about fighting is important too: when you fight, fight not to hurt one another but to grow in understanding and love. It's in the blessing we bring to others that we find we're blessed ourselves.

Now would you each like to try to write out this reading in your own words just as you would like to say it? What could each of you say to other engaged or married couples?

12. A reading from the first letter of John (3:18-24)

(St John tells us that it's only by showing that our love is real that we can know where we stand with God.)

Children,
our love must be not just words or mere talk,
but something active and genuine.
This will be the proof that we belong to the truth,
and it will convince us in his presence,
even if our own feelings condemn us,
that God is greater than our feelings and knows all things.
My dear friends,
if our own feelings do not condemn us,
we can be fearless before God,
and whatever we ask
we shall receive from him,
because we keep his commandments
and do what is acceptable to him.
His commandment is this,
that we should believe in the name of his Son Jesus Christ
and that we should love one another
as he commanded us.
Whoever keeps his commandments
remains in God, and God in him.
And this is the proof that he remains in us:
the Spirit that he has given us.

About the reading: Promise to be true

To hear someone say to you 'I love you' is great; but to hear it when you know that it's not sincere is one of the most hurtful experiences you can have. It's important to say 'I love you' but it mustn't stay at the talking stage. It's only when there's real active love there that we can be really honest and truthful with one another and with ourselves, and it's only in being really honest and truthful – in being 'children of the truth' – that we can have an easy conscience. Often, other people may know you better than you know yourself. It's only when you know that you love and are loved that you can find the courage to see yourself as you really are. But God knows us, and he knows our consciences, and he knows his own love is stronger than any accusations against us in our conscience. We needn't be afraid of God's presence – he knows us, and still he loves us!

God does hear our prayers. But our God is not a dispensing machine, where you can put in your money, and out pops the can of orange. You may come across promises like this: 'Say this prayer nine times a day for nine days, and leave nine copies in a church each day, and you will get your request. Never known to fail!' Certainly it is good to pray with perseverance; but a promise like this does not reflect the God that Jesus Christ tells of. Nor is our God one who can be bribed or blackmailed or forced. Our God is the God who is love, as you'll see in the next reading. When we live in love, we do not try to manipulate the other person. Rather, we receive the gift of the Spirit of love.

St John was a teenager when he first came to know Jesus. You can see from this letter that the love John found in Jesus was still very much alive when this letter was written many years later.

13. A reading from the first letter of John (4:7-12)

(St John tells us that we can't see God, but we can still know him – because God is love: your love!)

My dear friends,
let us love one another,
since love is from God
and everyone who loves is a child of God and knows God.
Whoever fails to love does not know God,
because God is love.
This is the revelation of God's love for us,
that God sent his only Son into the world

that we might have life through him.
Love consists in this:
it is not we who loved God,
but God loved us and sent his Son
to expiate our sins.
My dear friends,
if God loved us so much,
we too should love one another.
No one has ever seen God,
but as long as we love one another
God remains in us
and his love comes to its perfection in us.

About the reading: What difference do you make to me?

Take a few minutes off. Just relax, and think of the person you're planning to spend your married life with. If you like, form a picture in your mind – a clear, definite picture, of that person in a particular place at a particular time. It shouldn't be hard – so far!

Now think of the difference that person's love has made to you. How much it means to you: the happiness you have, and the sacrifices you make for one another; how much your love means to the other; how things are different for you both since you got to know and love one another; how it has affected your relationships with other people – at home, at work, friends, neighbours.

Now think of the difference it makes – or could make – to you to know that God loves you. Think of your experience of God – the ways you have met him; what he has done for you; what you do for him. He loves you. You are a child of God, no matter what your age. God is love.

How does God's love for you, and your love for him, affect your love for the person you're planning to marry? Try to be definite. Think of concrete ways in which the love between God and you makes a difference; think of particular cases or incidents. You may find this quite difficult. It may help if each of you just writes down your thoughts about each of the questions above. Or speak your thoughts about them into a tape recorder, while you're quite alone, without even the other person present. Then swap your thoughts, as I suggested with the exercise on the reading from Sirach on page 122. Take your time to read or listen to them; then talk.

Notice the love the reading speaks of. Sometimes people say something like this:

'The most important thing in being a Christian is to love God and our neighbour'. These are certainly important; but there's something even more basic: first of all 'it is not we who loved God, but God loved us and sent his son'. It's because we have known this that we want to bring that same love to one another; and then 'As long as we love one another, God remains in us...'.

God is love, and we are the children of God. Do the children take after the parent? Your love, with God's grace, will be growing as the years go by. Your love for one another in five or fifty years' time will not be just the same as your love for one another on your wedding day – if it were, there would be something wrong! Your relationship with God, too, and with Jesus Christ, will also continue to grow and develop. With the relationships growing and changing, you need never be short of something to talk about!

14. A reading from the book of Revelation (19:1, 5-9)

(St John sees the end of everything like a tremendous wedding feast that lasts forever. It's the wedding of Christ and his people, the Church; and we're all invited! Your wedding will bring you closer to that.)

I, John, heard what seemed to be the great sound of a huge crowd in heaven, singing, 'Alleluia! Salvation and glory and power to our God!' Then a voice came from the throne; it said, 'Praise our God, you servants of his and those who fear him, small and great alike.'

And I heard what seemed to be the voices of a huge crowd, like the sound of the ocean or the great roar of thunder, answering, 'Alleluia! The reign of the Lord our God Almighty has begun; let us be glad and joyful and give glory to God, because this is the time for the marriage of the Lamb. His bride is ready, and she has been able to dress herself in dazzling white linen, because her linen is made of the good deeds of the saints.'

The angel said, 'Write this: Blessed are those who are invited to the wedding feast of the Lamb.'

About the reading: Your invitation

Often a wedding brings together a whole crowd of people who haven't met for a long time – maybe even members of the one family; and there are so many things to talk about! And if they're in really good form, what a noise they can make – even in a church, a place where they normally wouldn't think of being noisy. Did you ever think of heaven as a noisy place?

Of course, there are many ways of thinking about heaven, and none of them can come near the real joy of it. This reading gives us some idea by talking of it like a great crowd for a wedding feast, and singing and shouting with joy. I think it means more than a picture of yourself on your own little cloud with your own little wings, playing your harp to yourself. Quite often in the Bible, the idea of God being married to his people is used, to help us understand how much he loves us and wants to be united with us.

It's a natural reaction with people to praise the bride and groom at a wedding – and not just at speeches! The word 'Alleluia' means something like 'come on, everyone – let's praise God!' The bride in this reading is the people of God, the Church, described as dressed as a bride. The Lamb is Jesus Christ, the Lamb of God, who gave his life for his people. We're all invited to the wedding feast. In the reading, of course, it's particularly about heaven as something ahead of us; but it says something about now, because we already belong to God's people. Your wedding is a part of that wedding feast, because God is Love. By living your marriage as Christians, you're bringing that wedding feast closer – in fact, you're even sharing in it already both as Christians and as a couple. You are blessed when you celebrate Mass and share in communion – 'Blessed are those who are called to share in his supper'.

May every meal you share in your home be a source of blessing to you; and may everyone whom you invite to share a meal at your table share in that blessing also.

GOSPEL ACCLAMATIONS

The Gospels tell us how much Jesus meant to the first Christians as their way of life; they tell it in the form of stories of his life and works. We always have a reading from one of the four Gospels. See which reading you like best. To mark how important the Gospel reading is for us, and to prepare us to take it to heart, we 'acclaim' or greet the reading. It is to be sung, if possible. Otherwise, it may be read by all or by one person; it may be omitted if not sung.

'Alleluia' is a phrase in Hebrew, which means 'Praise God!' We use it very much in the Easter season. As we prepare for Easter during Lent, we omit the word 'Alleluia'. It may be replaced by a phrase such as one of the following:

Praise to you, O Christ, king of eternal glory!
Praise and honour to you, Lord Jesus!
Glory and praise to you, O Christ!
Glory to you, O Christ; you are the Word of God!
Sing out with joy to God, our strength.

The Gospel Acclamation may be sung or spoken as follows:

Reader/Cantor: Alleluia! *(In Lent: phrase as above.)*
All: Alleluia! *(In Lent: phrase as above.)*

Reader/Cantor: (Choose one of the following)

1. God is love;
   let us love one another
   as God has loved us. *(1 John 4:8,11)*

2. As long as we love one another,
   God will live in us
   and his love will be complete in us. *(1 John 4:12)*

3. Anyone who lives in love
   lives in God
   and God lives in him. *(1 John 4:16)*

4. Everyone who loves
   is begotten by God
   and knows God. *(1 John 4:7)*

All: Alleluia! *(In Lent: phrase as above.)*

Gospel Readings

1. A reading from the holy Gospel according to Matthew (5:1-12)
(Jesus describes a very deep kind of happiness: a generous kind of happiness that nothing can take away.)

Seeing the crowds, Jesus went onto the mountain. And when he was seated his disciples came to him. Then he began to speak. This is what he taught them:

'How blessed are the poor in spirit:
the kingdom of heaven is theirs.
Blessed are the gentle:
they shall have the earth as inheritance.
Blessed are those who mourn:
they shall be comforted.
Blessed are those who hunger and thirst for uprightness:
they shall have their fill.
Blessed are the merciful:
they shall have mercy shown them.
Blessed are the pure in heart:
they shall see God.
Blessed are the peacemakers:
they shall be recognised as children of God.
Blessed are those who are persecuted in the cause of uprightness:
the kingdom of heaven is theirs.
Blessed are you when people abuse you and persecute you and speak all kinds of calumny against you falsely on my account.
Rejoice and be glad, for your reward will be great in heaven.'

***About the reading:* Recipes for happiness**

'Happily ever after' is the way we'd like to live, just like in the fairy stories when the hero marries his princess. If you read magazines or watch television or films, look out for the 'happily ever after' kind of story, and ask yourself what kind of happiness they tell you about. Then maybe you could each write out a list of the

things you think make for happiness in your marriage, and compare your two lists; see what you've agreed on, and what's different. Discuss between yourselves why you think various items are important, and see if you can agree on how to number them, beginning with the most important. You needn't expect to have the same list as any other couple would have! It doesn't matter how long you're married, or whether you're just planning it now – you can still make out your list together. Then keep the list – maybe even put it up on the wall where you can look at it often. After six months or a year, have another look together. Ask yourselves how far you've got; why you didn't manage to arrive at the same things yet; and whether some items on your list should be changed for the coming year!

Check your list against the list Jesus gives us. His isn't just for marriage – it's for any follower of his. Do his ideas strike you as being not very practical; as being the opposite of what you think; or as being very close to your ideas? Talk about his list together, and see where you agree or disagree with each other about what he means. Try to put his in an order of importance you can agree on. You could look at the list again, in six months or a year. Jesus doesn't promise an easy passage; he even promises persecution in the cause of right. But he does promise: 'Rejoice and be glad, for your reward will be great in heaven'. Could you write that at the end of your own list?

2. A reading from the holy Gospel according to Matthew (5:13-16)

(Reminds you that your happiness must go out beyond the two of you, to everyone you meet, if it is really to last.)

Jesus said to his disciples: 'You are salt for the earth. But if salt loses its taste, what can make it salty again? It is good for nothing, and can only be thrown out to be trampled under people's feet. You are light for the world. A city built on a hill-top cannot be hidden. No one lights a lamp to put it under a tub; they put it on the lamp-stand where it shines for everyone in the house. In the same way your light must shine in people's sight, so that, seeing your good works, they may give praise to your Father in heaven'.

About the reading: Demonstrations

Demonstrations and pickets and marches and strikes and protests and bombs and parades and ceremonies are ways of getting people to wake up and take notice of what the organisers want to say. If you see it on the television or on a newspaper, you'll at least notice that it's there, even if you don't agree with it; even more so if you get caught up in traffic on account of it! In fact, these kinds of things are often planned specially to disturb people and so that they'll get on the News. They don't want to be hidden.

Your wedding is a demonstration. You are the organisers. Whether you invite just a few, or hundreds of people, it's bound to succeed. It's a kind of demonstration that's 'recognised'. That's what a wedding is; if it's in a registry office, you're asking the State to recognise it; if it's in a church, you're asking the Church and the State to recognise it. It's not just going off to live together; you want to make a demonstration of your decision. You don't light a lamp and put it under a tub.

You are the light of the world. Let your light shine. Let it shine, not just on your wedding day, but forever. That way, you'll be an inspiration to a lot of others. The goodness of God will shine through your lives. You are the salt of the earth; the way you live will make life 'tasty', really worth living, for some other people – perhaps even for people you don't know. If you become 'tasteless', you'll be letting down not just yourselves, but others too. Can you think of a few people who were an inspiration to you in big ways or small ways? Tell each other about these people, and try to understand what your partner learned from them. Then maybe you could thank God together for all those people who inspired you in any way. May many other people praise and thank God for you, too, in the same way some day.

3. A reading from the holy Gospel according to Matthew (7:21, 24-29)
(A married couple needs somewhere to live. But it is also important to put your life itself on a firm foundation.)

(Shorter form: omit text in brackets.)
Jesus said to his disciples: 'It is not anyone who says to me, "Lord, Lord," who will enter the kingdom of heaven, but the person who does the will of my Father in heaven. Therefore, everyone who listens to these words of mine and acts on them will be like a sensible man who built his house on rock. Rain came down, floods rose, gales blew and hurled themselves against that house, and it did not fall: it was founded on rock. [But everyone who listens to these words of mine and does not act on them will be like a stupid man who built his house on sand. Rain came down, floods rose, gales blew and struck that house, and it fell; and what a fall it had!' Jesus had now finished what he wanted to

say, and his teaching made a deep impression on the people because he taught them with authority, unlike their own scribes.]

About the reading: *Ask an expert*

Getting a new television can be quite a bother, if the controls are quite different to the one you had before. Not to mention satellite or video recorder or DVD! It helps when you get to understand what the different buttons do. If you don't have the User's Handbook, or if it's difficult to understand, you may never find out how to do what you want it to do. Sometimes we just have to ask someone who knows, so we can listen and watch and learn for ourselves. Someone who speaks with the real authority that can only come from knowing; not the false authority that is just an abuse of power. If you are familiar with computers, and someone were to ask your advice about how to do something on a computer, that's fine. But if that person then ignores what you say – well, you won't be too surprised, perhaps, if things get in quite a mess.

People could recognise that Jesus knew what he was talking about. He taught with authority. We can recognise that too. It doesn't mean it's easy to take him at his word. But he's talking about you and me. Maybe it's easy enough when things are working fine; but when the winds and the rains and the floods come, what then? 'He wouldn't expect too much – he knows things are difficult.' But that's when we need to depend on his word more than ever. We can't afford not to. When do you call him in? When the whole thing is just about to collapse? (Of course, then you can blame him for not doing his job.) The time to build a strong foundation is in the fine weather. The time to get to know what Jesus says is now. Today.

4. A reading from the holy Gospel according to Matthew (19:3-6)

(Marriage is naturally for ever!)

Some Pharisees approached Jesus, and to put him to the test they said, 'Is it against the Law for a man to divorce his wife on any pretext whatever?' He answered, 'Have you not read that the Creator from the beginning made them male and female and that he said: "This is why a man leaves his father and mother and becomes attached to his wife, and the two become one flesh?" They are no longer two, therefore, but one flesh. So then, what God has united, human beings must not divide.'

About the reading: For ever and ever

If there were a law to say that if you like, you can believe that 2 and 2 makes 3 or 4, whichever you like, which would you pick? Maybe it sounds ridiculous to ask that: '4 of course', wouldn't you say? But then, there might be times when it would suit you better to say '3' – for instance, when you're paying a bill. What would you do then? With an impossible example, like this, it's easy enough to see that what matters is not what's convenient, but what you know is true.

There was a reason behind the question put to Jesus in this reading. One group said that a divorce could be given for any reason at all; another group said it could be given in a case of adultery. Jesus went deeper than both: he went back to the original plan. And so, for a Christian getting married, this is what is important. If it's God who unites you, nothing need ever divide you.

So what about divorce? And what about annulments from the Church? Aren't there some marriages that never work – that are a disaster? It's true. That's why preparation for marriage is so important. The break-up of such a close union between two people is the cause of tremendous suffering for both, and for children too. A divorce from a government authority means that the State says: 'You were married; now, as far as we're concerned, you're not'. When the Church 'dissolves' a marriage, what usually is the case is that the Church says: 'Although it seemed that you were married, we now recognise that it never really was a marriage, for these reasons…'. What the Church says about marriage arises from our concern, as followers of Christ, for people and for marriages. This is why, in the Church, we can be so concerned to help our people to prepare for marriage. This preparation takes place especially at home; also in school, clubs, and so on; and especially when you have come to make a choice in marriage. This concern doesn't stop with the wedding. Pray that the Church will always bring God's blessings to you all through your married life.

5. A reading from the holy Gospel according to Matthew (22:35-40)

(Real love is the most important thing you can put into practice in your life; it should be behind everything you do.)

To put Jesus to the test, one of the Pharisees put a question, 'Master, which is the greatest commandment of the Law?' Jesus said to him, 'You must love the Lord your God with all your heart, with all your soul, and with all your mind. This is the greatest and the first commandment. The second resembles it: You must love your neighbour as yourself. On these two commandments hang the whole Law, and the Prophets too.'

About the reading: The power behind the law

Whether you're engaged or married, you know that someone loves you enough to want to spend a lifetime with you. It's a tremendous thing to know. How does it make you feel? Does it make you feel privileged, or embarrassed? Do you reply with love, or with a feeling of annoyance at being tied down? When you're getting married, the answers would be plain enough: to feel privileged and to reply with love. The odd thing is that so often, when we think about God loving us, we've been inclined to feel: 'So what do I have to do now? Yes – keep a lot of commandments!'

When the lawyer asked Jesus the question in this reading, he would have been thinking of the 613 commandments of all kinds that experts in the Law counted up in their time. Jesus went right to the heart of the matter. The most important reply to God is love – to love with all your heart and soul and mind. Is this your reply to God?

And then Jesus did a strange thing. He added on a bit. Love your neighbour. Just as much as you love yourself.

He didn't say: 'Love any of your neighbours who love you'. Just 'Love'. Love doesn't have to be earned. Love is a gift. And it's on loving God and your neighbour that all the law depends.

It may seem strange to talk about commanding someone to love. (You'll find similar sayings in other readings from St John's Gospel, on pages 162 and 165.) After all, you can't always be sure how you're going to feel about a person, can you? How I feel may vary, depending on what time I got to bed last night, or on what the weather is like, or on what someone says to me, or on the state of my health.

It seems that what Jesus is speaking of is not about how I feel about other people. He's speaking of something more basic: how I decide to be towards other people. It's great, of course, when my feelings go along that way. But I can decide to act and speak with care and gentleness and patience and love, even at the times when I don't actually feel a warmth towards a person. Is this false, just pretending? No: it's saying that while feelings are an important and valuable part of my life, it is not feelings that control my life. I am far more than how I feel today. I take responsibility for what I do and say. And if I am a disciple of Jesus Christ, I want the wisdom and life of Jesus Christ within me to be the controlling Spirit in my life. That way, I can be really and truly free to love.

All the laws in the world won't make one person love another. But your love for a person will give you the power and courage and freedom to live all the laws of love – love for your husband or wife just as much as love for God.

6. A reading from the holy Gospel according to Mark (10:6-9)

(It is God who made man and woman for one another.)

Jesus said to them, 'From the beginning of creation God made them male and female. This is why a man leaves his father and mother, and the two become one flesh. They are no longer two, therefore, but one flesh. So then, what God has united, human beings must not divide.'

About the reading: Looking forward to a change

In my parents' house, one year, we took away a door between two rooms and removed the small step in the doorway. For a few months afterwards, we all found we were automatically stepping on the step that wasn't there anymore, and getting a surprise every time! Taking away the door and the step were easy enough. The hardest thing to change was the habit we had. There are so many small habits that we don't think of until we're disturbed. Habits like the order you have for putting on your clothes in the morning; or the way you like your dinner; or the friends you meet regularly. If you move house, you may even find yourself heading automatically towards your old home sometimes!

When you marry, you start a new life, but your habits don't leave you easily. You may leave your father and mother and live elsewhere, but it will take time to adjust your ways of thinking. From now on, you are closer to the person you marry than to your own parents, or brothers and sisters, or friends you work with or go out with.

It's important for parents to accept that their children will grow up and begin to make their own lives. It's important, too, for you to be prepared for this with any children you may have. It's important for your friends (if they are real friends) to accept your marriage, and to accept that from now on someone else is the person you centre your life on. No matter how much your friends may miss doing some of the things you did together, they will see that things have to change.

It's not that you have to break off with anyone; but your style of life has to change. You must have changed to some extent as you planned your marriage; it's important not to drift back to your old ways after the honeymoon. 'God unites you' doesn't mean just that you can get a bit of paper from the Church to say the wedding took place; it has to be worked out in every little corner of your lives, all your life long. It's not a 50-50 partnership; it's a complete merger. That's the challenge; that's the thrill. With God on your side you can do it.

7. A reading from the holy Gospel according to John (2:1-11)
(Jesus brings extra happiness at a wedding.)

There was a wedding at Cana in Galilee. The mother of Jesus was there, and Jesus and his disciples had also been invited. And they ran out of wine, since the wine provided for the feast had all been used, and the mother of Jesus said to him, 'They have no wine.' Jesus said, 'Woman, what do you want from me? My hour has not come yet.' His mother said to the servants, 'Do whatever he tells you.' There were six stone water jars standing there, meant for the ablutions that are customary among the Jews: each could hold twenty or thirty gallons.

Jesus said to the servants, 'Fill the jars with water,' and they filled them to the brim. Then he said to them, 'Draw some out now and take it to the president of the feast.' They did this; the president tasted the water, and it had turned into wine. Having no idea where it came from, though the servants who had drawn the water knew, the president of the feast called the bridegroom and said, 'Everyone serves good wine first and the worse wine when the guests are well wined; but you have kept the best wine till now.' This was the first of Jesus' signs: it was at Cana in Galilee. He revealed his glory, and his disciples believed in him.

About the reading: A friend worth having

If even half the stories that are told about Jesus are true, he must have been an extraordinary person. St John tells us this story, because he wants us to have some idea of how extraordinary Jesus was. And this is why we still tell this story today: because we believe that the same Jesus is alive with us today.

Mary and Jesus and his followers were invited to the wedding, so they must have been friends of the pair getting married. Nothing strange about that. But if you're a Christian you are a follower of his. Will he be a welcome guest at your wedding? Or will he be there just because you feel you have no choice – maybe like some relations you just 'have to' invite? Will you do your best to keep him out of it, except that you feel you 'have to' have the wedding in a church?

And what about afterwards? Jesus enjoyed being with friends, even when they couldn't figure him out at all. Does he feel welcome in your home?

The most extraordinary thing about it all is that we believe that he is really with us, and that we can get to know him. A good way is like in the story here: the bride and groom want to share their happiness with him. Nothing strange about that. But you can do the same: not just the happiness of your wedding day, but all that comes afterwards too. He's not just for emergencies – but often works quietly; at Cana, the bride and groom didn't know what was happening behind the scenes. He keeps the best wine until the time it's really needed. If you'll do whatever he tells you you will see his glory in your marriage.

8. A reading from the holy Gospel according to John (15:9-12)

(Jesus wants his own joy to be in us. Your happiness on your wedding day is a share in his joy – because you love one another.)

Jesus said to his disciples:
'I have loved you
just as the Father has loved me.
Remain in my love.
If you keep my commandments
you will remain in my love,
just as I have kept my Father's commandments
and remain in his love.
I have told you this
so that my own joy may be in you
and your joy be complete.
This is my commandment:
love one another,
as I have loved you.'

About the reading: Presents full of meaning

Take a few minutes off, just to think a bit. Think of each other. How much do you mean to each other? Imagine you're describing your fiancé or fiancée (or husband or wife) to a friend of yours abroad who has never met him or her. How would you describe him or her, not just looks, but personality, life story, etc?

Now, imagine that you could take your pick of anything you wanted in the whole world to give to the one with whom you want to live in love for the rest of your life. What would you choose as a gift, in order to make his or her joy complete?

Again, think of all you actually have now, or could do, as a gift: whether great or small, what would you give that would make his or her joy complete? And why? Words can say a lot, but they cannot say everything that a gift stands for. If words could say it all, we'd never need to give a gift! But words can help to bring home the deeper meaning of the gift. Some people have a special gift with words, perhaps in poetry or song – do you have such a poem or song or something else that seems to express what it is you want to say better than you can yourself?

Jesus says he wants his own joy to be in us, and our joy to be complete. As St John tells it in this reading, these are words of Jesus the night before he died. His gift to us is himself, even laying down his life so that we will know for sure that there is nothing, not even suffering and death, that can put a stop to his love for us. He wants us to be able to live in his love today and always.

That's what you do in giving yourselves to one another, in laying down your lives for one another, in your marriage. That's your gift to one another: a gift that goes far beyond words. That's why we have more than just words at a wedding. We have ceremony, ritual – actions to convey something of the deeper meaning. All the little things you do in love for one another convey something of that deeper meaning. They are a kind of language that goes beyond words: a language in which you want to tell the truth of your 'true love'. It's a holy language, a sacred language. And the act of 'making love' is part of that language which goes beyond love. (It's a language that can be cheapened by misuse, where sexual intercourse is just a casual or recreational activity, where it tells a lie: 'Last night meant nothing'.) Your total, lifelong gift of yourselves in marriage is the real language of true love.

9. A reading from the holy Gospel according to John (15:12-16)

(Jesus loved us enough to give his life for us. When you marry, you give the rest of your lives to each other.)

Jesus said to his disciples:
'This is my commandment:
love one another,
as I have loved you.
No one can have greater love
than to lay down his life for his friends.
You are my friends,
if you do what I command you.

I shall no longer call you servants,
because a servant does not know
the master's business;
I call you friends,
because I have made known to you
everything I have learnt from my Father.
You did not choose me,
no, I chose you;
and I commissioned you
to go out and to bear fruit,
fruit that will last;
so that the Father will give you
anything you ask him in my name.'

About the reading: What's in a name?

We had no say in the names we were given shortly after we were born. But now, in marrying, if you live under one name, you say something important by living under the one name; you say that you want to make your two single lives into one joint life. You don't join up just for convenience; you join up because you're very close friends – you're lovers. Naturally, you won't always agree on everything; but there is such a bond of trust and closeness that your life is in the one name.

It's important that Jesus calls us friends. That's how he genuinely feels about us, and he really means it. He even wants to share with us all he learned from his Father. But if we're to get to know him that well, we have to learn to listen to him, so that we can be sure we get his meaning. It's when we sincerely want to do that, that we can really use his name, and call ourselves Christian.

You can practise listening to each other like that, too. Try this, for instance. Have a discussion together on something pretty important like how you get on with your in-laws, or bringing up your children.

Decide which one of you will speak first. Take a few moments to think, and the first person speaks for a minute or so about it. Then the other person can articulate some thoughts. But before adding anything new, you must repeat in your own words what you understand the first person to mean, until the first person is satisfied that you have got it fully. Then you can say what you want to say, and the same rule applies: the person who spoke first now has to repeat in different words what you have said until you're happy that you've got your meaning across. When you try this you may find it's much harder to keep to the one rule than you think. A referee might be useful to help you keep it!

When you are sure you really want to understand one another, you can be sure your friendship will last. When you really want to understand Jesus, you can be sure of your friendship with Jesus. And you can be sure he'll stick by you in all your wants.

10. A reading from the holy Gospel according to John (17:20-26)
(Jesus prayed at the Last Supper that his followers would be completely united. May you two be so united as husband and wife that it will be plain to everyone that your love comes from God.)

(Shorter form: omit text in brackets.)
Jesus raised his eyes to heaven and said:
'Father, I pray not only for these
but also for those
who through their teaching will come to believe in me.
May they all be one,
just as, Father, you are in me and I am in you,
so that they also may be in us,
so that the world may believe it was you who sent me.
I have given them the glory you gave to me,
that they may be one as we are one.
With me in them and you in me,
may they be so perfected in unity
that the world will recognise that it was you who sent me
and that you have loved them as you have loved me.
[Father,
I want those you have given me
to be with me where I am,
so that they may always see my glory
which you have given me
because you loved me
before the foundation of the world.
Father, Upright One,

the world has not known you,
but I have known you,
and these have known
that you have sent me.
I have made your name known to them
and will continue to make it known,
so that the love with which you loved me may be in them,
and so that I may be in them.']

About the reading: Two into one goes

After three years going around with someone, you'd know each other pretty well. You'd have a lot of memories and experiences in common. What about the future?

After three years with the twelve, Jesus knew them pretty well. They had come through a lot together. Now, looking to the future, Jesus had one special prayer for them – that they would be one. Not just one as a good team working together, but one as closely as he himself and his Father are one. And he prayed not just for them, but for everyone who would come to believe in him afterwards. In other words, for you and me.

Look ahead ten years. How would you like your friends to be able to talk about you as husband and wife in ten years' time? To be able to say: 'Just look at them! Look how close they are to one another! They really have something going for them'. For Jesus, the 'something going for you' can be your faith in him, and people can recognise it. You have faith in each other. Your faith in Jesus can help your faith in each other to grow stronger. Even when you're not actually together, you still have faith in each other, because in a very real way you are always together: you are one. Even when Jesus doesn't seem to be with you, you can still believe in him, because he is in you and you are in him. He has given you and me his glory, his oneness with his Father.

He even prays that we may always see that glory he's talking about. He does not pray impossible prayers. When he wants something, it isn't just wishful thinking. He's prepared to do something about it. If we are willing to work with him, he will do it for us. May his glory and his love be seen in your marriage.

Homily

After the readings we have some reflections to gather together some of the significant thoughts of the Word of God for this celebration.

This leads in to what we do next – the exchange of consent between bride and groom, before the Church gathered here with you today, and before those whom you have asked to witness for the Church and the world what you are doing here.

CELEBRATION OF MARRIAGE

For this part of the celebration, it is good that bride and groom take a central position, where those present can witness what they do and say. To have their backs to the congregation scarcely does justice either to their role, or to the role of the congregation who, with the presiding priest or deacon, are the Church before whom the couple exchange their consent The priest or deacon is the minister who simply asks and receives the consent of the couple on behalf of the Church; bride and groom are themselves the ministers of the sacrament of marriage, and should be both visible and audible to the congregation. How this is done will vary with the design of the place in which the wedding is celebrated.

The Rite for Ireland

There are four parts to this rite. In each part, you have choices.

1. *Address and questions to the couple.*
2. *Exchange of consent.*
3. *Explanatory rites (ring or rings; gift or gifts; prayer of the couple).*
4. *General Intercessions ('Prayer of the Faithful').*

Another choice: As well as the choices offered in the English language, you will find on page 175 the rite as used in the Irish language. A translation into

English is on page 247. This is drawn from Irish sources. Look in particular at the Solemn Calling (Gairmglaoch) *and the Prayer of the Faithful* (Guí an Phobail).

The rites for Scotland, England and Wales are given in Appendix 3 on page 258.

Note: *Words marked with an asterisk * at various places in the rite may be omitted in particular cases, for example, if the couple are advanced in years.*

The parts said by various people in the Liturgy of Marriage are marked:
M: Minister – priest or deacon
B: Bride
G: Bridegroom
Where 'N' is used, the personal name of the relevant person is said.

Address and Questions to the Couple

Choose A, B or C. See also Irish language rite. There is a sample alternative on page 255.

A

M: Dear children of God, you have come to this church so that the Lord may seal your love in the presence of the priest and this community. Christian marriage is a sacred union which enriches natural love. It binds those who enter it to be faithful to each other for ever; it creates between them a bond that endures for life and cannot be broken; it demands that they love and honour each other (that they accept from God the children he may give them, and bring them up in his love). To help them in their marriage, the husband and wife receive the lifelong grace of the sacrament.

Is this your understanding of marriage?
B & G: It is.

B

M: Dear children of God, you have come to this church so that the Lord may seal your love in the presence of the priest and this community. Christ blesses this love. He has already consecrated you in baptism; now, by a special sacrament, he strengthens you to fulfil the duties of your married life.

N. and N., you are about to celebrate this sacrament. Have you come here of your own free will and choice and without compulsion to marry each other?

B & G: We have.

M: Will you love and honour each other in marriage all the days of your life?

B & G: We will.

[**M:* Are you willing to accept with love the children God may send you, and bring them up in accordance with the law of Christ and his Church?

B & G: We are.]

C

M: Dear children of God, you have come today to pledge your love before God and before the Church here present in the person of the priest, your families and friends.

In becoming husband and wife you give yourselves to each other for life. You promise to be true and faithful, to support and cherish each other until death, so that your years together will be the living out in love of the pledge you now make. May your love for each other reflect the enduring love of Christ for his Church.

As you face the future together, keep in mind that the sacrament of marriage unites you with Christ, and brings you, through the years, the grace and blessing of God our Father. Marriage is from God: he alone can give you the happiness which goes beyond human expectation, and which grows deeper through the difficulties and struggles of life.

Put your trust in God as you set out together in life. Make your home a centre of Christian family life. (In this you will bequeath to your children a heritage more lasting than temporal wealth.)

The Christian home makes Christ and his Church present in the world of everyday things. May all who enter your home find there the presence of the Lord: for he has said: 'Where two or three are gathered together in my name, there am I in the midst of them'.

Now, as you are about to exchange your marriage vows, the Church wishes to be assured that you appreciate the meaning of what you do, and so I ask you:

Have you come here of your own free will and choice and without compulsion to marry each other?
B & G: We have.

M: Will you love and honour each other in marriage all the days of your life?
B & G: We will.

[*M:* Are you willing to accept with love the children God may send you, and bring them up in accordance with the law of Christ and his Church?
B & G: We are.]

Exchange of Consent

Choose A, B, C or D. See also Irish language rite. The assisting minister invites you in each case to declare your consent. Then, in the first and fourth forms, you say everything yourselves. In the second form, you also say everything, but with less to say. In the third form, the minister puts a question to each of you, and you just answer the question. Remember: your first inclination need not be your final choice! There seems to be no reason why the groom would necessarily come first in speaking, if you agree that it should be the other way round!

M: I invite you then to declare before God and his Church your consent (*or:* your decision) to become husband and wife.

A

G: N., do you consent to be my wife?
B: I do. Do you, N., consent to be my husband?
G: I do. I take you as my wife,
and I give myself to you as your husband –
B: I take you as my husband,
and I give myself to you as your wife –
(together, hands joined:)
Both: to love each other truly,
for better, for worse,
for richer, for poorer,
in sickness and in health,
till death do us part. *(Or:* all the days of our life.*)*
M: What God joins together man must not separate.
May the Lord confirm the consent that you have
given, and enrich you with his blessings.

B

(Bride and groom join hands.)
G: I, N., take you N., as my wife,
for better, for worse
for richer, for poorer,
in sickness and in health,
till death do us part. *(Or:* all the days of our life.*)*
B: I, N., take you N., as my husband,
for better, for worse,
for richer, for poorer,
in sickness and in health,
till death do us part. *(Or:* all the days of our life.*)*
M: What God joins together man must not separate.
May the Lord confirm the consent that you have
given, and enrich you with his blessings.

C

(Bride and groom join hands.)

M: N., do you take N., as your wife,
for better, for worse,
for richer, for poorer,
in sickness and in health,
till death do you part?
(Or: all the days of your life?*)*

G: I do.

M: N., do you take N., as your husband,
for better, for worse,
for richer, for poorer,
in sickness and in health,
till death do you part?
(Or: all the days of your life?*)*

B: I do.

M: What God joins together man must not separate.
May the Lord confirm the consent that you have
given, and enrich you with his blessings.

D

G: N., do you consent to be my wife?

B: I do.

B: N., do you consent to be my husband?

G: I do

(Bride and groom join hands.)

Both: We take each other as husband and wife
and promise to love each other truly
for better, for worse,
for richer, for poorer,
in sickness and in health,
till death do us part. *(Or:* all the days of our life.*)*

M: What God joins together man must not separate.
May the Lord confirm the consent that you have
given, and enrich you with his blessings.

Explanatory Rites

Choose A, B, C or D. See also Irish language rite.

A ring is a traditional symbol and reminder of love: a circle without beginning or end.

A

M: May the Lord bless this ring (these rings) which will be the sign of your love and fidelity.
All: Amen.

B

M: Lord, bless N. and N., and consecrate their married life.
May this ring (these rings) be a symbol of their faith in each other, and a reminder of their love.
Through Christ, our Lord.
All: Amen.

C

M: Lord bless this ring (these rings).
Grant that those who wear them may always be faithful to each other. May they do your will and live in peace with you in mutual love. Through Christ, our Lord.
All: Amen.

D

M: Almighty God, bless this ring (these rings), symbol(s) of faithfulness and unbroken love.
May N. and N. always be true to each other, may they be one in heart and mind, may they be united in love forever, through Christ, our Lord.
All: Amen.

The bridegroom places the bride's ring on her ring finger. He may say:

G: N., wear this ring as a sign of our faithful love.
In the name of the Father, and of the Son, and of the Holy Spirit.
or N., wear this ring as a sign of our love and fidelity.

The bride may place a ring on the bridegroom's finger. She may say;

B: N., wear this ring as a sign of our faithful love.
In the name of the Father, and of the Son, and of the Holy Spirit.
or N., wear this ring as a sign of our love and fidelity.

If you wish, the groom may give some small gift of value, for example, a piece of gold or silver, to the bride; or each may give a small gift to the other. This is a sign that from now on they share everything. Giving the gift, you may say:

'I give you this gold/silver/gift, as a token of all I possess.'

Prayer of the Newly Married Couple

The couple are recommended to say together the following prayer, or a similar one which they may choose or prepare themselves:

We thank you, Lord,
and we praise you
for bringing us
to this happy day.

You have given us to each other.
Now, together, we give ourselves to you.

We ask you, Lord:
make us one in your love:
keep us one in your peace.

Protect our marriage.
Bless our home.
Make us gentle.
Keep us faithful.
And when life is over
unite us again
where parting is no more
in the kingdom of your love.

There we will praise you
in the happiness and peace
of our eternal home.
Amen.

Alternatively, the prayer may be said before or after the prayer after communion, page 212.

Continue now to page 180: Prayer of the Faithful.

Gnás an Phósta le linn Aifrinn

(English language translation on page 247)

Deasghnáth iomlán ann féin atá sa téacs seo. Ba cheart é a úsáid leis féin. Tar éis an homaile:

Gairmghlaoch

Sagart: Bíodh a fhios agaibh go bhfuilimid bailithe anseo i láthair ar an… lá… de… de bhliain ár dTiarna… (an… lá… den ghealach) chun glacadh le rún pósta A. agus A.
chun aontachta agus aontíos;
chun grá agus dílseachta;
chun measa agus onóra;
chun carthanachta agus measarthachta;
chun misnigh agus féile;

chun móraigeantachta agus maithiúnais;
chun uaisleachta agus maorgachta;
chun buaine go bás.
I láthair Dé agus na hEaglaise,
in ainm na Tríonóide RóNaofa
agus i síocháin na Páise;
in onóir na Maighdine Muire, Máthair Dé,
na Naomh Aspal agus na Naomh uile;
faoi bhrí na Sacraiminte Naofa;
iarraim oraibh an bhfuil sibh toilteanach
glacadh lena chéile mar fhear agus mar bhean chéile?

Lánúin: Táimid toilteanach.

(Sagart: An nglacfaidh sibh le cibé leanaí a chuirfidh Dia chugaibh agus an dtógfaidh sibh iad de réir dhlí Chríost agus na hEaglaise?

Lánúin: Glacfaimid agus tógfaimid.)

Dearbhú Toilteanais

Sagart: Tugaim cuireadh daoibh dearbhú os comhair Dé agus na hEaglaise gurb é bhur dtoil é go ndéanfaí fear céile agus bean chéile díbh.

Beireann siad greim láimhe ar a chéile. Deir an fear:

F: Glacaimse, A., leatsa, a A., mar bhean chéile,
más fearr sin, más measa,
más tinn nó más slán,
go scara an bás sinn. (*nó* gach lá dár saol.)

Deir an bhrídeog:

B: Glacaimse A., leatsa a A., mar fhear chéile,
más fearr sin, más measa,
más tinn nó más slán,
go scara an bás sinn (*nó* gach lá dár saol).

Tar éis don lánúin a dtoil dá chéile a chur in iúl, deir an sagart:

S: An ní a cheanglaíonn Dia, ná scaoileadh duine é.
Go neartaí Dia leis an toil atá tugtha agaibh dá chéile
agus go mbronna sé a bheannacht oraibh go fial.

Beannú na bhFáinní

Sagart: Beannaigh ✠ A. agus A., a Thiarna, agus déan a saol pósta a choisrcacan.
Go raibh an fáinne (na fáinní) seo mar chomhartha ar a ndílseacht agus go gcuire sé (said) i gcuimhne dóibh a ngrá dá chéile.
Sin é ár nguí chugat trí Chríost ár dTiarna.

Pobal: Amen.

Croitheann an sagart uisce coisricthe ar na fáinní.

Cuireann an fear fáinne na mná ar a fáinneog. Ní miste dó a rá:

F: AA., caith an fáinne seo mar chomhartha ar ár ngrá agus ar ár ndílseacht.
In ainm an Athar agus an Mhic agus an Spioraid Naoimh.
Amen.

Ní mistc don bhrídcog fáinnc an fhir a chur ar a fháinncog siúd. Ní mistc di a rá:

B: AA., caith an fáinne seo mar chomhartha ar ár ngrá agus ar ár ndílseacht.
In ainm an Athar agus an Mhic agus an Spioraid Naoimh.
Amen.

An Tabhartas

Ní miste don fhear ór agus airgead a thabhairt dá bhean chéile, á rá:

F: Tugaim duit an t-ór agus an t-airgead seo,
comharthaí ar mo mhaoin shaolta uile.

nó ní miste don fhear agus don bhrídeog bronntanais bheaga shiombalacha a thabhairt dá chéile, á rá:

A A., tugaim an bronntanas seo duit,
i ngeall ar mo mhaoin shaolta uile.

Guí an Phobail ***(An ceann seo nó ceann eile)***

Sagart: Guímis: Ag an bpósadh a bhí i Cána bhí Rí na nGrás ann i bpearsa. Iarraimis air an lánúin seo a bheannú, faoi mar a bheannaigh sé an bhainis úd i nGailile.

Brídeog: A Íosa, a Mhic Muire,
Déan trócaire orainn.

Pobal: A Rí na Rí,
A Dhia na nDúl.

Fear: Bí um thús ár slí,
Bí um chríoch ár saoil.

Pobal: A Rí na Rí,
A Dhia na nDúl.

Brídeog: Bí ag múscailt ár mbeatha,
Bí ag dubhadh ár lae.

Pobal: A Rí na Rí,
A Dhia na nDúl.

Fear: Bí romhainn agus linn,
Go deireadh ár ré.

Pobal: A Rí na Rí,
A Dhia na nDúl.

Brídeog: Coisric sinn,
Croí agus crann.

Pobal: A Rí na Rí,
A Dhia na nDúl.

Fear: Coisric sinn,
Corp agus cuid.

Pobal: A Rí na Rí,
A Dhia na nDúl.

Brídeog: Coisric sinn,
Croí agus cré.

Pobal: A Rí na Rí,
A Dhia na nDúl.

Fear: Ár gcroí is ár gcré,
Gach lá duit féin.

Pobal: A Rí na Rí,
A Dhia na nDúl.

Athair na Brídeoige:
Bua ratha daoibh:
Bua mac is iníonacha daoibh:
Bua mara is tíre daoibh.

Máthair na Brídeoige:
Bua grá daoibh:
Bua dílse daoibh:
Bua Flaithis daoibh:
Bua lae is oíche daoibh.

Athair an Fhir:
Maitheas mara daoibh:
Maitheas talaimh daoibh:
Maitheas Neimhe daoibh.

Máthair an Fhir:
Gach lá sona daoibh:
Gan lá dona daoibh:
Onóir is urraim daoibh:
Grá gach duine daoibh.

Sagart: A Dhia shíoraí uilechumhachtaigh, dearc anuas ar do sheirbhísigh A. agus A. atá aontaithe sa phósadh anseo inniu, agus tabhair dóibh, as ucht a ngrá dá chéile, go mairfidh a ngrá duitse go buan.
Sin é ár nguí chugat trí Chríost ár dTiarna.

Pobal: Amen.

Leanann an tAifreann ar aghaidh. Féach 183.

General Intercessions

(Prayer of the Faithful)

(for use in Ireland, Scotland, England and Wales)

You want your wedding day to be happy. But you don't want to keep that happiness for yourselves alone. Happiness is something to be shared – not just today but all your life. So now we have prayers for yourselves, but also for other married people: for those at the wedding; for those who are unhappy; for all the people you will want to share your happiness with; for the Church; and for all the world. You can make up your own prayers, as you would like them yourselves. Usually there are about five, but you can have as many as you like. You could also ask some person to read them; or you could ask a number of people to read one each; or, if the church is suitable, you could leave it open to people to make their own prayers aloud, from their places.

Whoever is preparing these prayers should remember that each intention is not a prayer in itself, but an invitation to the people that they themselves will pray for the intention. So the usual form will not be addressed to God but to the people: 'Let us pray for…' or 'Let us ask the Lord for…'. Then the people themselves take a few moments to pray for that intention in silence. So it should not be hurried through – allow people time to think and pray at each intention. This can be difficult for the person leading until he or she gets used to the idea that even ten or fifteen seconds of silence with each petition is not too long before continuing with 'Let us pray to the Lord', and the people then responding aloud. It is good if the people's response can be sung.

The support and love of Mary can fittingly be included among these intentions if desired, but the recitation of the 'Hail Mary' is not part of the Prayer of the Faithful.

See also Irish language rite on page 178, with translation in English on page 249.

The priest introduces and concludes the Prayer of the Faithful.

Sample Formulae

Some of these intercessions may be selected. Others may be devised. In determining the content of the Prayer of the Faithful it should be kept in mind that intercessions may be made for the Church, for civil authorities, for those oppressed by various needs, for the salvation of all humanity as well as for the couple being married.

In place of 'Let us pray to the Lord', 'Lord, hear our prayer'; a different form of response may be used, for example:
Lord, hear us.
Lord, graciously hear us.

M: Let us pray, now,
for the newly married couple,
for married people everywhere,
for the Church and for the world.

Reader 1: For N. and N.,
that the Lord,
who brought them to this happy day,
will keep them forever
in fidelity and love,
let us pray to the lord.
All: Lord, hear our prayer.

Reader 2: For the parents of N. and N., for their friends
and all who have helped them
to become husband and wife,
let us pray to the Lord.
All: Lord, hear our prayer.

Reader 3: For the world and its peoples,
that the Lord may bless them with his peace
and the protection of his love,
let us pray to the Lord.
All: Lord, hear our prayer.

Reader 4: For our community and our families,
who welcome Christ into their lives;

that they may learn to receive him
in the poor and suffering people of this world,
let us pray to the Lord.

All: Lord, hear our prayer.

Reader 5: For God's Church,
the Bride of Christ,
that it may be united in faith and love,
let us pray to the Lord.

All: Lord, hear our prayer.

Reader 6: For all who are victims of injustice,
and for those deprived of love and affection,
let us pray to the Lord.

All: Lord, hear our prayer.

Reader 7: For married couples everywhere
that their lives will be an example to the world
of unity, fidelity and love,
let us pray to the Lord.

All: Lord, hear our prayer.

Reader 8: For those who mourn, while we are rejoicing,
that in their suffering and loneliness
they may experience the strength of God's support,
let us pray to the Lord.

All: Lord, hear our prayer.

Reader 9: For the faithful departed
and especially for those
whom we, ourselves, have loved,
that God will one day unite us again
in the joys of our eternal home,
let us pray to the Lord.

All: Lord, hear our prayer.

M: God our Father,
you are the creator of all that is good.
Listen to these, our prayers,
which we make with trust in Jesus Christ, your Son, our Lord.

All: Amen.

The Profession of Faith, the Creed, is said on Sundays and solemn feasts; it may also be said in solemn local celebrations. It follows the Prayer of the Faithful.

LITURGY OF THE EUCHARIST

Preparation of the gifts and altar

Having prayed, listened and done many things already, we come to the Eucharist. 'Eucharist' is a Greek word that means 'Thanksgiving'. Together we all, and the two of you for the first time as husband and wife, thank God for giving us love – both the love he gave us in Jesus Christ, and the love you know today among those who care about you, especially between the two of you now and for the rest of your life together. In a mysterious way, it's all the one love.

Before the bread and wine for the Eucharist are brought forward, the altar itself can also be prepared by some of the congregation: it could be bare till now, while we celebrated the Liturgy of the Word and the Liturgy of Marriage; so the cloth(s) for the altar could be spread, and candles and missal placed, before the bread and wine are presented by some of the congregation and accepted by the priest.

The bread and wine are now presented. They are not just bread and wine – they stand for yourselves, for all your food, all your happiness and love, all your work and troubles in the past, present and future, in fact, for everything that life means to you.

If you wish to have items that are not gifts, but significant symbols of your life and faith, to be placed near the altar, this is done more appropriately at the beginning of the celebration rather than now.

The gifts are not restricted to bread and wine; other items may be brought forward to prepare the altar for the Liturgy of the Eucharist: cloth, candles, missal, chalice, etc. You could also arrange for extra gifts to be given to those in need, as a sign that as a couple and as a congregation, we are thinking not just of ourselves. As many people as necessary may be involved.

How you want to do this depends on a number of things, like the layout of the church and the length of the bride's dress! Some suggestions:

1. *The table with the gifts may be close by or further down the church.*
2. *The two of you, or your best man and bridesmaid, can go down and bring the gifts directly up to the priest.*
3. *Your parents or any others could do so.*
4. *You could ask some others to bring them up; the two of you turn around and receive them, and then you turn back to give them to the priest.*

Priest: Pray, brothers and sisters, that our sacrifice may be acceptable to God, the almighty Father.
All: May the Lord accept the sacrifice at your hands for the praise and glory of his name,
for our good, and the good of all his Church.

The length of the bride's dress is a factor.

The priest says a prayer over the gifts to dedicate them to God. There are three prayers suggested. Choose A, B or C.

A

This asks for God's blessing on you always.

Lord,
accept our offering
for this newly-married couple, N. and N.
By your love and providence you have
brought them together;
now bless them all the days of their life.

B

This asks for God's fatherly protection.

Lord,
accept the gifts we offer you
on this happy day.
In your fatherly love
watch over and protect N. and N.,
whom you have united in marriage.

C

We pray that your wedding Mass, in remembering what Christ has done, will inspire you both.

Lord,
hear our prayers
and accept the gifts we offer for N. and N.
Today you have made them one in the sacrament of marriage.
May the mystery of Christ's unselfish love,
which we celebrate in this eucharist,
increase their love for you and for each other.
We make our prayer, as always, through Christ our Lord.

Eucharistic Prayer

We now come to the part of the Mass that may seem to have least to do with you – we remember what God did long ago in sending his Son to us. In fact, it has a lot to do with you. When you celebrate a wedding anniversary, you'll be celebrating not just something that happened years ago, but something that is still alive and means a lot to you. We celebrate what Jesus Christ did because he's still alive today. Often, when the Bible speaks of God's love for humanity, it compares it to the love of a husband and wife. Your love, in a mysterious way, is God's love for you. Your marriage is itself a reminder of God and what he has done for us!

We begin the Eucharistic Prayer with a Preface – a prayer of thanks. The Preface leads into the 'Sanctus' – a song uniting us with all the angels and saints in praising God. This in turn leads us into the central prayer of thanksgiving, the Eucharistic Prayer, in grateful memory of Jesus, and which finishes with the 'Great Amen'. The dialogue at the start of the Preface, and the Preface itself, may be sung, just as the 'Holy Holy' is recommended to be sung.

Priest: The Lord be with you.
All: And also with you.
Priest: Lift up your hearts.
All: We lift them up to the Lord.
Priest: Let us give thanks to the Lord our God.
All: It is right to give him thanks and praise.

There are three wedding Prefaces to choose from, unless you choose the Fourth Eucharistic Prayer which has its own proper Preface.

1

In the first Preface, we thank God for the gift of marriage, and for making it holy.

Father, all-powerful and ever-living God,
we do well always and everywhere to give you thanks.

By this sacrament your grace unites man and woman
in an unbreakable bond of love and peace.

You have designed the chaste love of husband and wife
for the increase both of the human family
and of your own family born in baptism.

You are the loving Father of the world of nature;
you are the loving Father of the new creation of grace.
In Christian marriage you bring together the two orders of creation:
nature's gift of children enriches the world
and your grace enriches also your Church.

Through Christ the choirs of angels
and all the saints
praise and worship your glory.
May our voices blend with theirs
as we join in their unending hymn of praise:

> Holy, holy, holy Lord, God of power and might,
> Heaven and earth are full of your glory.
> Hosanna in the highest.
> Blessed is he who comes in the name of the Lord.
> Hosanna in the highest.

2

In the second Preface we thank God for giving us his 'covenant' – for wanting to love us; and for making marriage a sign of his covenant.

Father, all-powerful and ever-living God,
we do well always and everywhere to give you thanks
through Jesus Christ our Lord.

Through him you entered into a new covenant with your people.
You restored man to grace in the saving mystery of redemption.

You gave him a share in the divine life
through his union with Christ.
You made him an heir of Christ's eternal glory.

This outpouring of love in the new covenant of grace
is symbolised in the marriage covenant
that seals the love of husband and wife
and reflects your divine plan of love.

And so, with the angels and all the saints in heaven,
we proclaim your glory
and join in their unending hymn of praise:

> Holy, holy, holy Lord, God of power and might,
> Heaven and earth are full of your glory.
> Hosanna in the highest.
> Blessed is he who comes in the name of the Lord.
> Hosanna in the highest.

3

The third Preface concentrates on the idea of love.

Father, all-powerful and ever-living God,
we do well always and everywhere to give you thanks.

You created man in love to share your divine life.
We see his high destiny in the love of husband and wife,
which bears the imprint of your own divine love.

Love is man's origin,
love is his constant calling,
love is his fulfilment in heaven.
The love of man and woman
is made holy in the sacrament of marriage,
and becomes the mirror of your everlasting love.

Through Christ the choirs of angels
and all the saints
praise and worship your glory.
May our voices blend with theirs
as we join in their unending hymn of praise:

> Holy, holy, holy Lord, God of power and might,
> Heaven and earth are full of your glory.
> Hosanna in the highest.
> Blessed is he who comes in the name of the Lord.
> Hosanna in the highest.

You may choose Eucharistic Prayer 1, 2 or 3, each of which has a few lines of prayer for bride and groom on their wedding day; or you may choose Eucharistic Prayer 4, which comes with its own special Preface. If appropriate, you may choose another approved Eucharistic Prayer.

Eucharistic Prayer 1

The first Eucharistic Prayer is known as the Roman Canon.

We come to you, Father,
with praise and thanksgiving,
through Jesus Christ your Son.
Through him we ask you to accept and bless
these gifts we offer you in sacrifice.

We offer them for your holy catholic Church,
watch over it, Lord, and guide it;
grant it peace and unity throughout the world.
We offer them for N. our Pope,
for N. our bishop,
and for all who hold and teach the catholic faith
that comes to us from the apostles.

Remember, Lord, your people,
especially those for whom we now pray. *(Silence)*

Remember all of us gathered here before you.
You know how firmly we believe in you
and dedicate ourselves to you.
We offer you this sacrifice of praise
for ourselves and those who are dear to us.
We pray to you, our living and true God,
for our well-being and redemption.

In union with the whole Church
we honour Mary,
the ever-virgin mother of Jesus Christ our Lord and God.
We honour Joseph, her husband,
the apostles and martyrs
Peter and Paul, Andrew
and all the saints.
May their merits and prayers
gain us your constant help and protection.

Father, accept this offering
from your whole family
and from N. and N., for whom we now pray.
You have brought them to their wedding day:
grant them (the gift and joy of children and)
a long and happy life together.

Bless and approve our offering;
make it acceptable to you,
an offering in spirit and in truth.
Let it become for us
the body and blood of Jesus Christ,
your only son, our Lord.

The day before he suffered
he took bread in his sacred hands
and looking up to heaven,
to you his almighty Father,
he gave you thanks and praise.
He broke the bread,
gave it to his disciples, and said:
Take this, all of you, and eat it:
This is my body which will be given up for you.

When supper was ended,
he took the cup.
Again he gave you thanks and praise,
gave the cup to his disciples, and said:
Take this, all of you, and drink from it:
this is the cup of my blood,
the blood of the new and everlasting covenant.
It will be shed for you and for all
so that sins may be forgiven.
Do this in memory of me.

Let us proclaim the mystery of faith. *(See page 201)*

Father, we celebrate the memory of Christ, your Son.

We, your people and ministers,
recall his passion,
his resurrection from the dead,
and his ascension into glory;
and from the many gifts you have given us
we offer to you, God of glory and majesty,
this holy and perfect sacrifice:
the bread of life
and the cup of eternal salvation.

Look with favour on these offerings
and accept them as once you accepted
the gifts of your servant Abel,
the sacrifice of Abraham, our father in faith,
and the bread and wine offered by your priest, Melchisedech.
Almighty God,
we pray that your angel may take this sacrifice
to your altar in heaven.
Then as we receive from this altar
the sacred body and blood of your Son,
let us be filled with every grace and blessing.

Remember, Lord, those who have died
and have gone before us marked with the sign of faith,
especially those for whom we now pray. *(Silence)*
May these, and all who sleep in Christ,
find in your presence
light, happiness and peace.

For ourselves, too, we ask
some share in the fellowship of your apostles and martyrs,
with John the Baptist, Stephen, Matthias, Barnabas
and all the saints.
Though we are sinners,
we trust in your mercy and love.
Do not consider what we truly deserve,
but grant us your forgiveness.

Through Christ our Lord
you give us all these gifts.
You fill them with life and goodness,
you bless them and make them holy.

Through him,
with him,

in him,
in the unity of the Holy Spirit,
all glory and honour is yours,
almighty Father,
for ever and ever.

All: Amen.

Eucharistic Prayer 2

This is the shortest and simplest of the Eucharistic Prayers.

Lord, you are holy indeed,
the fountain of all holiness.
Let your Spirit come upon these gifts to make them holy,
so that they may become for us
the body and blood of our Lord, Jesus Christ.

Before he was given up to death,
a death he freely accepted,
he took bread, and gave you thanks.
He broke the bread,
gave it to his disciples, and said:
Take this all of you, and eat it:
This is my body which will be given up for you.

When supper was ended, he took the cup.
Again he gave you thanks and praise,
gave the cup to his disciples, and said:
Take this, all of you, and drink from it:
this is the cup of my blood,
the blood of the new and everlasting covenant.
It will be shed for you and for all
so that sins may be forgiven.
Do this in memory of me.

Let us proclaim the mystery of faith. *(See page 201)*

In memory of his death and resurrection,
we offer you, Father, this life-giving bread,
this saving cup.
We thank you for counting us worthy
to stand in your presence and serve you.
May all of us who share in the body and blood of Christ
be brought together in unity by the Holy Spirit.

Lord, remember your Church throughout the world;
make us grow in love,
together with N. our Pope,
N., our bishop, and all who minister to your people.
Remember also, Lord, N. and N.,
whom you have brought to their wedding day,
that, by your grace,
they may always live in mutual love and peace.
Remember our brothers and sisters
who have gone to their rest
in the hope of rising again;
bring them and all the departed
into the light of your presence.
Have mercy on us all;
make us worthy to share eternal life
with Mary, the virgin mother of God,
with the apostles, and with all the saints
who have done your will throughout the ages.
May we praise you in union with them,
and give you glory
through you Son, Jesus Christ.

Through him,
with him,
in him,

in the unity of the Holy Spirit,
all glory and honour is yours,
almighty Father,
for ever and ever.

All: Amen.

Eucharistic Prayer 3

This is the prayer you may be most familiar with – it is very often used on Sundays and holy days.

Father, you are holy indeed,
and all creation rightly gives you praise.
All life, all holiness comes from you
through your Son, Jesus Christ our Lord,
by the working of the Holy Spirit.
From age to age you gather a people to yourself,
so that from east to west
a perfect offering may be made
to the glory of your name.
And so, Father, we bring you these gifts.
We ask you to make them holy by the power of your Spirit,
that they may become the body and blood
of your Son, our Lord Jesus Christ,
at whose command we celebrate this eucharist.

On the night he was betrayed,
he gave bread and gave you thanks and praise.
He broke the bread, gave it to his disciples and said:
Take this, all of you, and eat it:
this is my body which will be given up for you.

When supper was ended, he took the cup.
Again he gave you thanks and praise,

gave the cup to his disciples, and said:
Take this, all of you, and drink from it:
this is the cup of my blood,
the blood of the new and everlasting covenant.
It will be shed for you and for all
so that sins may be forgiven.
Do this in memory of me.

Let us proclaim the mystery of faith. *(See page 201)*

Father, calling to mind the death your Son endured for our salvation,
his glorious resurrection and ascension into heaven,
and ready to greet him when he comes again,
we offer you in thanksgiving this holy and living sacrifice.

Look with favour on your Church's offering,
and see the Victim whose death has reconciled us to yourself.
Grant that we, who are nourished by his body and blood,
may be filled with his Holy Spirit,
and become one body, one spirit in Christ.

May he make us an everlasting gift to you
and enable us to share in the inheritance of your saints,
with Mary, the virgin mother of God;
with the apostles, the martyrs,
Saint N. and all your saints,
on whose constant intercession we rely for help.

Lord, may this sacrifice,
which has made our peace with you,
advance the peace and salvation of all the world.
Strengthen in faith and love your pilgrim Church on earth;
your servant, Pope N., our bishop N., and all the bishops,
with the clergy and the entire people your Son has gained for you.
Father, hear the prayers of the family you have

gathered here before you.
Strengthen in the grace of marriage N. and N.,
whom you have brought to their wedding day;
keep them faithful throughout their lives
to the covenant they have sealed in your presence.
Unite to yourself all your children
now scattered over the face of the earth.
Welcome into your kingdom our departed brothers and sisters,
and all who have left this world in your friendship.
We hope to enjoy for ever the vision of your glory,
through Christ our Lord, from whom all good things come.

Through him,
with him,
in him,
in the unity of the Holy Spirit,
all glory and honour is yours
almighty Father,
for ever and ever.

All: Amen.

Eucharistic Prayer 4

Instead of choosing one of the wedding Prefaces with one of the above three prayers, you may choose this Eucharistic Prayer with its own special Preface. It is another long prayer and is the one that tells best of all what God has done for us in offering us his covenant of love.

Father in heaven,
it is right that we should give you thanks and glory:
you alone are God, living and true.
Through all eternity you live in unapproachable light.
Source of life and goodness, you have created all things,
to fill your creatures with every blessing

and lead all men to the joyful vision of your light.
Countless hosts of angels stand before you to do your will;
they look upon your splendour
and praise you, night and day.
United with them,
and in the name of every creature under heaven,
we praise your glory as we sing (say):

> Holy, holy, holy Lord, God of power and might,
> heaven and earth are full of your glory.
> Hosanna in the highest.
> Blessed is he who comes in the name of the Lord.
> Hosanna in the highest.

Father, we acknowledge your greatness:
all your actions show your wisdom and love.
You formed man in your own likeness
and set him over the whole world
to serve you, his creator,
and to rule over all creatures.
Even when he disobeyed you and lost your friendship
you did not abandon him to the power of death,
but helped all men to seek and find you.
Again and again you offered a covenant to man,
and through the prophets taught him to hope for salvation.
Father, you so loved the world
that in the fullness of time you sent your only Son to be our Saviour.
He was conceived through the power of the Holy Spirit,
and born of the Virgin Mary,
a man like us in all things but sin.
To the poor he proclaimed the good news of salvation,
to prisoners, freedom,
and to those in sorrow, joy.
In fulfilment of your will
he gave himself up to death;

but by rising from the dead,
he destroyed death and restored life.
And that we might live no longer for ourselves but for him,
he sent the Holy Spirit from you, Father,
as his first gift to those who believe,
to complete his work on earth
and bring us the fullness of grace.

Father, may this Holy Spirit sanctify these offerings.
Let them become the body and blood of Jesus Christ our Lord
as we celebrate the great mystery
which he left us as an everlasting covenant.

He always loved those who were his own in the world.
When the time came for him to be glorified by you, his heavenly Father,
he showed the depth of his love.

While they were at supper,
he took bread, said the blessing, broke the bread
and gave it to his disciples, saying:
Take this, all of you, and eat it:
this is my body which will be given up for you.

In the same way, he took the cup, filled with wine.
He gave you thanks, and giving the cup to his disciples, said:
Take this, all of you, and drink from it:
this is the cup of my blood,
the blood of the new and everlasting covenant.
It will be shed for you and for all
so that sins may be forgiven.
Do this in memory of me.

Let us proclaim the mystery of faith. *(See page 201)*

Father, we now celebrate this memorial of our redemption.
We recall Christ's death, his descent among the dead,
his resurrection, and his ascension to your right hand;
and, looking forward to his coming in glory,
we offer you his body and blood,
the acceptable sacrifice
which brings salvation to the whole world.

Lord, look upon this sacrifice which you have given to your Church;
and by your Holy Spirit, gather all who share this bread and wine
(*or:* this one bread and one cup)
into the one body of Christ, a living sacrifice of praise.

Lord, remember those for whom we offer this sacrifice,
especially N. our Pope,
N. our bishop, and bishops and clergy everywhere.
Remember those who take part in this offering,
those here present and all your people,
and all who seek you with a sincere heart.

Remember those who have died in the peace of Christ
and all the dead whose faith is known to you alone.

Father, in your mercy grant also to us, your children,
to enter into our heavenly inheritance
in the company of the Virgin Mary, the Mother of God,
and your apostles and saints.
Then, in your kingdom, freed from the corruption of sin and death,
we shall sing your glory with every creature through Christ our Lord,
through whom you give us everything that is good.

Through him,
with him,
in him,
in the unity of the Holy Spirit,

all glory and honour is yours,
almighty Father,
for ever and ever.

All: Amen.

The Mystery of Faith

In every Eucharistic Prayer after telling what Jesus did at the last supper, we remember what he asked us to do; we proclaim the mystery of our faith in Jesus who has died and is risen. There are four acclamations suggested:

1. *We proclaim that Jesus really did die, but that he is now alive again, because death could not hold him; and that he will come again to his people – the same Jesus who died and rose for us.*

   Christ has died,
   Christ is risen,
   Christ will come again.

2. *We proclaim that in dying, Jesus set us free from the power of death. Even though we die, death need have no 'sting', because we are his, and because we already share his risen life. He is so important to us that we call on him (with urgency!) to come again.*

   Dying you destroyed our death,
   rising you restored our life.
   Lord Jesus, come in glory.

3. *We proclaim the death of Jesus every time we take the bread and cup at Mass. This would be strange, even morbid, if we didn't know that he is Lord – that the Father has glorified him; so we now look forward to his coming in glory.*

When we eat this bread and drink this cup,
we proclaim your death, Lord Jesus,
until you come in glory.

4. *We see the mystery of Christ in his cross and resurrection. He brings a freedom that no one else in the world can bring. Our faith is that he is 'Saviour' – the one who saves the world.*

Lord, by your cross and resurrection
you have set us free.
You are the Saviour of the world.

Communion Rite

We begin our preparation for Communion by praying the 'Lord's Prayer'. Some couples choose to pray this prayer in Irish. If you do so, and if there are some present who do not speak Irish, they could be invited to pray the prayer in their own language at the same time.

We are all of the one family, and God is our Father, so we pray to him now with confidence, as Jesus taught:

All: Our Father, who art in heaven,
hallowed be thy name;
thy kingdom come;
thy will be done on earth as it is in heaven.
Give us this day our daily bread;
and forgive us our trespasses
as we forgive those who trespass against us;
and lead us not into temptation,
but deliver us from evil.

Or, in Irish:
Ár nAthair, atá ar neamh,
Go naofar d'ainm.

Go dtaga do ríocht.
Go ndéantar do thoil ar an talamh
mar a dhéantar ar neamh.
Ár n-arán laethúil tabhair dúinn inniu,
agus maith dúinn ár bhfiacha
mar a mhaithimidne d'ár bhféichiúna féin.
Agus ná lig sinn i gcathú,
ach saor sinn ó olc.

Nuptial Blessing (Ireland)

(For Scotland, England and Wales, see Appendix 3, p. 267)

After the 'Our Father', the prayer beginning 'Deliver us, O Lord, from every evil…' is omitted; instead we have the Nuptial Blessing for the newly married couple. If one or both of the parties will not be receiving communion, the phrase in the invitation to the first three prayers, referring to the sacrament of Christ's body and blood, is omitted. Choose 1, 2, 3 or 4; or Nuptial Blessing in Irish on p. 208.

1

This is a beautiful prayer for all your future together.

Let us ask God to bless N. and N., now married in Christ, and unite them in love,
(through the sacrament of his body and blood).

All pray silently for a short while.

God our Father, creator of the universe,
you made man and woman in your own likeness,
and blessed their union.
We humbly pray to you for this bridegroom and bride,
today united in the sacrament of marriage.

May your blessing come upon them.
May they find happiness in their love for each other,
[be blessed in their children,*]
and enrich the life of the Church.

May they praise you in their days of happiness,
and turn to you in times of sorrow.
May they know the joy of your help in their work,
and the strength of your presence in their need.
May they worship you with the Church
and be your witnesses in the world.
May old age come to them in the company of their friends,
and may they reach at last the kingdom of heaven.

We ask this through Christ our Lord.

2

We remember here that it is God who made us men and women.

Let us ask God to bless N. and N., now married in Christ, and unite them in love,
(through the sacrament of his body and blood).

All pray silently for a short while.

Father, you created the universe
and made man and woman in your own likeness.
You gave woman as companion to man,
so that they should no longer be two, but one flesh,
teaching us that those you have so united may never be separated.

Father, you have sanctified marriage in a mystery so holy
that it is a sign of the union of Christ and the Church.
Look with love upon N., as she asks your blessing.
May she live in peace with you

and follow the example of those women
whose lives are praised in the scriptures.

May N. place his trust in her
and see her as his companion.
May he always honour her
and love her as Christ loves the Church.

Father, keep this husband and wife strong in faith
and true to your commandments.
May they be faithful to each other,
examples of Christian living,
and witnesses of Christ.
[Bless them with children and help them to be good parents.*]
And, after a long and happy life together,
may they enjoy the company of your saints in heaven.

We ask this through Christ our Lord.

3

This prayer tells of God's covenant of love with his people,
and of your covenant of love with each other.

Let us pray to the Lord for N. and N.,
who, as they begin their married life,
come to God's altar to deepen their love
(by sharing in the body and blood of Christ).

All pray silently for a short while.

Father, you created man and woman in your own image
and united them in body and heart
so that they might fulfil your plan for the world.
To reveal your loving design,
you made the union of man and wife

a sign of the covenant between you and your people;
through the sacrament of marriage you perfect this union,
and make it now a sign of Christ's love for his bride the Church.
Lord, bless this husband and wife and protect them.
Grant that as they live this sacrament
they may learn to share with each other the gifts of your love.
May they become one in heart and mind
as witnesses to your presence in their marriage.
[Bless them with children
who will be formed by the gospel and
have a place in your family in heaven.*]
May N. be a good wife [and mother*],
caring for her home,
faithful to her husband,
generous and kind.
May N. be a good husband [and a devoted father*]
gentle and strong,
faithful to his wife,
and a careful provider for his household.
Father, grant that, as they now come as man and wife to your altar,
they may one day share your feast in heaven.
We ask this through Christ our Lord.

4

This form develops the thoughts, using words and ideas from scripture.

We call God our Father. Let each of us now ask him, in silence, to bless these his children as they begin their married life.

All pray silently for a short while.

Father, from you every family in heaven and on earth takes its name.
You made us.
You made all that exists.
You made man and woman like yourself in their power to know and love.

You call them to share life with each other, saying 'It is not good for man to be alone'.
(You bless them with children to give new life to your people,
telling them: 'Increase and multiply, and fill the earth.'*)
We call to mind the fruitful companionship of Abraham,
our father in faith, and his wife Sarah.
We remember how your guiding hand brought Rebecca and Isaac together,
and how through the lives of Jacob and Rachel you prepared
the way for your kingdom.
Father, you take delight in the love of husband and wife,
that love which hopes and shares, heals and forgives.

We ask you to bless N. and N. as they set out on their new life.
Fill their hearts with your Holy Spirit,
the Spirit of understanding, joy, fortitude and peace.

Strengthen them to do your will, and in the trials of life to bear the cross with Christ.
May they praise you during the bright days, and call on you in times of trouble.
[May their children bring them your blessing, and give glory to your name.*]
Let their love be strong as death,
a fire that floods cannot drown,
a jewel beyond all price.
May their life together give witness to their faith in Christ.
May they see long and happy days
and be united forever in the kingdom of your glory.

We ask this through Christ our Lord.

5

Beannú an Phósta (English language translation in Appendix I, p. 251)

Sagart Iarraimis ar Dhia a bheannacht a chur ar A. agus A. agus iad a aontú le chéile ina ghrá.

Guíonn cách os íseal ar feadh tamaill bhig. Ansin leathann an sagart a lámha amach agus deir:

A Dhia, ár nAthair, cruthaitheoir na cruinne,
chum tú an duine de chré na talún
agus shéid ina phollairí anáil na beatha;
ar an gcaoi sin rinn tú anam beo den duine.
Agus dúirt tú: 'Ní maith é an duine a bheith leis féin.
Déanfaidh mé céile cúnta a dhiongmhála dó.'
Agus chuir tú suan trom ar an duine,
agus ina shuan dó, bhain tú easna as agus chuir feoil
ina timpeall.
An easna a bhain tú as an duine,
rinne tú bean aisti, agus thug chun an duine í.
Dúirt an duine ansin: 'Is cnámh de mo chnámhsa í seo
ar deireadh, agus is feoil de m'fheoilse í.
Tabharfar bean uirthi
mar gur baineadh as an bhfear í.'
Uime sin, fágann an fear a athair agus a mháthair
agus cloíonn sé lena mhnaoi,
agus déantar aon fheoil amháin díobh.
Agus bheannaigh tú iad, á rá leo:
'Bígí torthach, agus téigí i líonmhaire
agus líonaigí an talamh agus cuirigí smacht air.'
Dá bhrí sin, a Thiarna Dia,
bronn do bheannacht go fial
ar do sheirbhísigh A. agus A. anseo i láthair.
Beannaigh iad mar do bheannaigh tú
Ábram agus Sára,
Ísac agus Rebecca,
Sacharía agus Éilís,

Ióchaim agus Anna.
Cumhdaigh iad, a Thiarna,
mar a chumhdaigh tú Noa ón díle,
an triúr ón bhfoirnéis lasrach,
Ísac ón gclaíomh,
agus Pobal Mhaois ón daorsmacht san Éigipt.
Féach go ceansa ar do chumhal A.
Go gcaithe sí a saol faoi shíocháin leatsa
agus go leana sí i gcónaí sampla na mban a mholtar sa scrioptúr naofa.
Go raibh sí go soilbhir lena fear ar nós Raícheal;
go raibh sí críonna fearacht Rebecca;
go raibh saol fada faoi dhílseacht aici mar a bhí ag Sára.
Bua crutha di;
bua gutha di;
bua sláinte di;
bua áille di;
bua grá di;
bua grásta di;
go gcuire A. a iontaoibh inti
agus go raibh sí mar chompánach aige.
Go raibh meas aige uirthi i gcónaí,
agus grá aige di, mar atá ag Críost dá Eaglais.
A Athair,
coimeád an lánúin seo láidir sa chreideamh
agus dílis do d'aitheanta.
Go raibh siad dílis dá chéile;
go raibh siad ina n-eiseamláir den bheatha Chríostaí
agus go dtuga siad fianaise ar Chríost.
Go bhfeice siad sliocht a sleachta
agus tar éis dóibh saol fada sona a chaitheamh le chéile
go mbaine siad aoibhneas
as comhluadar do naomh ar neamh.
Sin é ár nguí chugat trí Chríost ár dTiarna.

Pobal Amen.

Sign of Peace

You are familiar with the sign of peace – a sign of friendship and love between people celebrating Mass, before they receive Communion. Customs and people vary; you could discuss it with the priest. It shows that our love for God must also be shared with neighbours; in fact, it shows that God has broken down all the barriers between us.

We give this sign (if you decided to have it) before we share in the one bread at Communion. It should not be just a stiff, formal gesture, but a warm sign of genuine friendship, and each person can decide to make it that. For instance, an obvious sign of love between bride and groom would be a kiss, and others could give whatever sign would be appropriate to them. Further, the bride and groom, or the best man and bridesmaid, or all together, could go to the guests to give them the sign of peace. People can feel free to move out of their places to go over to others, and maybe especially to people they don't know. Introducing oneself to a stranger is a sign of friendship. People who are not used to it may feel very strange, and tend just to whisper because they're in the church, and at Mass; but everyone can use their normal tone of voice.

Priest: Lord Jesus Christ, you said to your apostles:
I leave you peace, my peace I give you.
Look not on our sins, but on the faith of your Church,
and grant us the peace and unity of your kingdom
where you live for ever and ever.
All: Amen.
Priest: The peace of the Lord be with you always.
All: And also with you.
Priest: Let us offer each other the sign of peace.

According to local custom, the bride and bridegroom, and all present, offer each other an appropriate sign of peace and unity.

Communion

You'll be sharing the rest of your lives together. If possible, a very good way to experience and celebrate your unity with one another and with the rest of the followers of Jesus, the people who are the Body of Christ, is to receive Communion together. Later you may be cutting the wedding cake for many to share as a sign of their sharing in the celebration. Here, the bread of life is now broken as a sign that we are all called to share in this celebration of unity, while all sing or say:

Lamb of God, you take away the sins of the world:
    have mercy on us.
Lamb of God, you take away the sins of the world:
    have mercy on us.
Lamb of God, you take away the sins of the world:
    grant us peace.

All pray silently for a while.

Priest: This is the Lamb of God
who takes away the sins of the world.
Happy are those who are called to his supper.
All: Lord, I am not worthy to receive you,
but only say the word and I shall be healed.

Before the wedding day, talk with the priest about receiving Communion from the chalice at the wedding Mass: how to go about it, and how many may receive the chalice. Jesus Christ is not divided: he is living, and to receive Communion in the form of the eucharistic bread alone is to receive the full living Christ; similarly to receive the eucharistic wine alone; but, as the General Instruction on the Roman Missal says: 'The sign of communion is more complete when given under both kinds, since in that form the sign of the eucharistic meal appears more clearly. The intention of Christ that the new and eternal covenant be ratified in his blood is better expressed, as is the relation of the eucharistic banquet to the heavenly banquet'.

If there has not been singing during or after Communion, all may sing or read aloud a short 'Communion antiphon', a verse for reflection. Three are suggested:

A
Christ loved the Church, and gave himself up for her that he might present to himself a bride holy and without blemish.
(Eph 5:15.27)

B
A new commandment I give to you, that you love one another as I have loved you, says the Lord.
(John 13:34)

C
I will bless the Lord at all times, his praise always on my lips. Taste and see that the Lord is good. He is happy who seeks refuge in him.
(Ps 33:1.8)

After Communion, there is usually a short silence to pray about what the celebration means, and how you will carry it forward into your life.

If you wish to say the 'Prayer of the Newly Married Couple' (page 174), and have not done so in the Marriage Rite, you may do so here before or after the 'Prayer after Communion'.

1

Lord,
in your love
you have given us this eucharist
to unite us with one another and with you.
As you have made N. and N.
one in the sacrament of marriage
(and in the sharing of the one bread and the one cup),
so now make them one in love for each other.

2

Lord,
we who have shared the food of your table
pray for our friends N. and N.,
whom you have joined together in marriage.
Keep them close to you always.

May their love for each other
proclaim to all the world
their faith in you.

3

Almighty God,
may the sacrifice we have offered
and the eucharist we have shared
strengthen the love of N. and N.,
and give us all your fatherly aid.

Each prayer is made through Christ, our Lord.

CONCLUDING RITE

The register may be signed here and now in or near the sanctuary by the bride and groom, by the witnesses, and by the priest or deacon: preferably not on the altar, but on another table.

Any final words may be said now.

Solemn Blessing – Ireland

We have a solemn blessing of the bride and bridegroom; you may choose the form you wish. This is followed in each case by a blessing of all the people.

P: The Lord be with you.
All: And also with you.

1

P: May God, the eternal Father, keep you steadfast in your love.
All: Amen.
P: May you have [children to bless you*],

friends to console you,
and may you live in peace with all.

All: Amen.

P: May you bear witness among people to the love of God.
May the suffering and the poor find you generous
and welcome you one day into our Father's kingdom.

All: Amen.

P: May the peace of Christ ever dwell in your home.
May the angels of God protect it.
And may the holy family of Nazareth
be its model and inspiration.

All: Amen.

P: And may almighty God bless you all,
the Father, ✠ and the Son, and the Holy Spirit.

All: Amen.

2

P: May God, the almighty Father, grant you his joy;
[may he bless you in your children.*]

All: Amen.

P: May Jesus Christ, the Son of God, in his mercy
help you in good times and in bad.

All: Amen.

P: May the Holy Spirit of God
always fill you with his love.

All: Amen.

P: And may almighty God bless you all,
the Father ✠ and the Son, and the Holy Spirit.

All: Amen.

3

P: The Lord Jesus was present at the wedding in Cana;
today may he bless you and your families and friends.

All: Amen.

P: He loved his Church to the end;
may he fill your hearts to overflowing with his love.

All: Amen.

P: May he give you the grace to bear witness to his resurrection,
and look forward to his coming with hope and joy.

All: Amen.

P: May the peace of Christ ever dwell in your home;
may the angels of God protect it,
and may the holy family of Nazareth
be its model and inspiration.

All: Amen.

P: And may almighty God bless you all,
the Father, ✠ and the Son, and the Holy Spirit.

All: Amen.

4

(Translation in English on page 254)

Ní miste don sagart an gnás seo a leanas a chleachtadh. Le linn na beannachta bíonn Crois Bhríde ina láimh dheis ag an sagart. Gearrann sé fíor na Croise Naofa ar an lánúin agus ar na daoine léi. Ansin, tugann sé an Chrois don bhrídeog. De réir an tsean-nóis cuireann an bhrídeog Crois Bhríde ar bhalla a tí gach Lá 'le Bríde i rith a saoil mar bhean phósta.

Sagart: Síocháin an Athar libh,
Síocháin Chríost libh,
Síocháin an Spioraid libh,
Gach lá agus oíche. Amen.

Pobal: Gach lá agus oíche. Amen.

Sagart: Coimirce an Athar oraibh,
Coimirce Chríost oraibh,
Coimirce an Spioraid oraibh,
Gach lá agus oíche de bhur saol. Amen.

Pobal: Gach lá agus oíche de bhur saol. Amen.

Sagart: Beannacht an Athar oraibh,

Beannacht Chríost oraibh,
Beannacht an Spioraid oraibh,
Go coróin na beatha síoraí. Amen.

Pobal: Go coróin na beatha síoraí. Amen.

Sagart: Bail ó Dhia oraibh ó Shamhain go Lá 'le Bríde,
ó Lá 'le Bríde go Bealtaine,
ó Bhealtaine go Lúnasa,
is ó Lúnasa go Samhain;
is go mbeannaí Dia uilechumhachtach sibh,
Athair, ✠ Mac agus Spiorad Naomh.

Pobal: Amen.

Sagart: Go dté sibh slán faoi shíocháin Chríost.

Pobal: Buíochas le Dia.

SENDING FORTH

We are now sent forth, having heard the word of life and strengthened by the bread of life: each of us to live a life of love, whether married or single, and to bring that love to the world as we give thanks to God at all times.

M: The Mass is ended; go in peace.
or: Go in the peace of Christ.
or: Go in peace to love and serve the Lord.

All: Thanks be to God.

(Or: Ireland)

Sagart: Tá an tAifreann thart. Imigí faoi shíocháin.
nó: Go dté sibh slán faoi shíocháin Chríost.
nó: Imigí faoi shíocháin
chun grá agus seirbhís a thabhairt don Tiarna.

Pobal: Buíochas le Dia.

If the register has not yet been signed, this may be done now.

Then follows the formal or informal procession from the church! Have someone pre-arranged to check that nobody has left anything behind in the church. If you prepared special leaflets or booklets for the wedding, make sure someone collects them: it is courtesy to leave the church and grounds clean and tidy. If offerings have not already been given, have someone do so now.

There are some further ideas in the following pages: remember, a wedding is a day, a marriage is a lifetime! Every blessing to you both.

A checklist for the wedding may be found on page 290.

AS YOU CONTINUE THE DAY'S CELEBRATION

After the wedding ceremony in the church, you may be having a simple or elaborate reception for your guests. In some ways, the church ceremony and the reception afterwards are very similar.

In the church ceremony, there were a lot of things said, which express the meaning of your wedding day. At your reception, it is likely that there will be a lot of things said too – apart from the casual talk, there may be speeches to mark the occasion. And, just like at a church ceremony, the speaking may not always be of the highest quality; but this does not take from the occasion!

There were symbolic actions in the church ceremony. At your reception, you may also have symbolic actions. Some couples have a formal 'Entrance Procession', perhaps with music, where everyone stands as the occasion commences. You may have an 'Opening Prayer', the 'Grace before Meals', and candles on the table. You may have a formal cutting of the wedding cake. If your wedding ceremony was in the context of a Wedding Mass, there was the 'Breaking of Bread' before Communion. Your guests are invited to share in the one wedding cake, just as, at Mass, we share in the one Bread of Life in Communion (although, sadly, because of Christians being divided, there may not have been full 'communion' here).

If you have a wedding candle (or wedding candle plus two), why just use it in the church? You could have someone bring it to your reception and put it on your table. Let the staff know beforehand that you'll be doing this. As you begin the meal, if you have someone to ask all to stand for a prayer, grace before the meal, this person could say something like: 'Please stand, as the bride and groom light their wedding candle, and then *(Name of person)* will lead us in grace'. As you will, no doubt, keep the candle at home, you could light it on your wedding anniversaries over the coming years.

When the time comes at the reception for you to do the formal cutting of the wedding cake, perhaps you would like that the best man ask your guests to join you in prayer for a moment. Then you, the bride and groom, go to stand at the cake, and pray together. Here is a suggestion. You may like to prepare a prayer in your own words.

Best man: *Ladies and gentlemen,*
let us stand as the bride and groom
ask a blessing on our sharing in this cake.
(All pause for a quiet moment.)

B & G: *Most loving God of all creation,*
we thank you for what we have already shared today.
We thank you for this wedding cake.
We are about to share in it as a symbol of our sharing in this celebration of joy.
Bless all of us who share in its sweetness, so that we may know the sweetness of being united with one another in love and in peace.
We pray that our sharing brings a blessing too on those who are absent today.
We pray that our married life may bring a blessing to the world around us until we are united again at the wedding banquet in your kingdom for ever and ever.

All: *Amen.*

Best man: *The bride and groom will now cut the cake!*

May every meal you share throughout your married life strengthen the blessing of this day for you.

PART V

WHAT HAPPENS NOW?

YOUR WEDDING GOES ON

You celebrate your wedding day, but your wedding keeps going on afterwards – wedding [illegible] wedding [illegible] one another as [illegible] and [illegible] parents are [illegible] you [illegible] after [illegible] how much [illegible] after your [illegible]

You have a lot to do [illegible] to [illegible] inside your [illegible]

[illegible] much [illegible] have many [illegible] not [illegible] to reach [illegible] to arrive at the [illegible] always open between [illegible] ourselves and God.

[illegible] the wedding is [illegible] album. Parts of it [illegible] Some parts can still be of great use [illegible] the readings is good. After six months [illegible] of marriage, you could [illegible] something [illegible] and is never out of date [illegible] is his word. If you [illegible] your marriage to go over the readings again, maybe [illegible] week, it will add a lot to your [illegible]

YOUR WEDDING GOES ON

You celebrate your wedding day, but your wedding keeps going on afterwards – wedding yourselves to each other. It's a lifelong wedding: a joining, a pledging. Don't be shy of referring to one another as husband and wife. The word 'partners' is often used as a general term, and I'm sure you will certainly be that; but so much more as well. I hope that the chapter early on in this book, 'Introducing Christian Marriage', will be of some help to you in appreciating how much more. Maybe you would read it again a few months after your wedding; see if you understand it differently then!

You have a lot to do. You've got to get used to the idea of living for each other, not just with each other. But you're not there to imprison each other. The real kind of prison is the one that's inside you, keeping yourself into yourself: prejudice and selfishness. Love breaks you out and makes you free. Real freedom is the kind that's inside you.

It will come slowly – sometimes it will seem much too slow; but it has to grow, and it has growing pains. A day comes – maybe many times – when you must choose each other over again, choose yourselves as the people you will have become by then. You're not getting married to settle down – you're getting married to travel together, onwards. God doesn't want either of you to arrive at his home alone. Keep the lines of communication always open between you. And keep them always open, too, between yourselves and God, who is love.

I hope you won't think this book is no use after the wedding, or that it's only for storing away with the photograph album. Parts of it, of course, won't affect you in the same way. Some parts can still be of great use. The work you put into choosing the readings is good. After six months or a year or two of marriage, you could get something quite new out of them. God is never out of date; neither is his word. If you start early on in your marriage to go over the readings again, maybe once a week, it will add a lot to your life together. The readings go from pages 111 to 166. After that you could go on to the Bible itself.

Eventually you might like to come together with a few other married couples for this kind of discussion and prayer, or make contact with one of the organisations for the enrichment of married life, mentioned in the 'contacts' section on page 242.

It's not a matter of adding another job to all the things you have to do. It's a matter of deciding priorities: what are the most important things to do. The fact that in recent times the Bible hasn't been given an important place in many Christian marriages doesn't mean that it's not important.

The forms of prayer that we give on page 227 could be helpful; or you could pick or devise your own form. One popular traditional form has been the family Rosary; there are many other possibilities too. It doesn't matter whether it's short or long; what does matter is that it shouldn't be just a formality, but real praying. A husband and wife can be a tremendous help to each other in their faith.

Getting married is not an escape from anything, nor is it a reward for anything. Love has its high points, but you can't always live at high points. You can't live all the time in the same state of excitement as on your wedding day – ordinary everyday life is a normal part of being married too. And the fact that you've had a wedding isn't automatically going to keep things running smoothly. A lot of things in the world will have changed in five or ten years' time. Your relationship can't be just the same after five or ten years as it was on your wedding day.

Getting married doesn't automatically make anyone more religious, even if you marry in a church. There's more to being a Christian than just getting baptised. There's more to being a Christian family than just marrying in a church. But if you share together the work on the wedding ceremony, it's a good start for sharing your faith through the years. Wherever you make your home, you take your place in the local parish: not just a piece of territory, but a group of people. It is a good idea to introduce yourself to a priest in your new parish. In many parishes, it's impossible for a priest to keep in touch with people moving in and out of the area, so if you leave it to him, it may be a long time before he knows you exist! Belonging to a parish can give you one way of sharing the happiness of your marriage with others. Marriage has to do with love – but not a love that you keep closed up between you. If you have children, it will have gone that far, but it can't just stop there either. Marriage won't satisfy all the needs of any person – it's the centre, but it has to spread out and grow. Your wedding is the start of this.

You join hands at your wedding. The wedding ceremony is over in a day, but you travel the rest of your lives hand in hand. When you go hand in hand, you go with God too. That's not all over and done with at your wedding day – it lasts all your life. God's help, his love, his grace, is not just to fall back on when you're in trouble, he's there all the time.

It can be difficult for a priest to keep in touch with people moving in and out of the area.

How much are you worth to each other? You learn what you are worth by the value another person puts on you. You know the value God puts on you.

The grace of our Lord, Jesus Christ, and the love of God, and the fellowship of the Holy Spirit be with you.

Two Wedding Mementoes

On your wedding day, you take time out to do something important together; and you share food. Is that it?

Your memories are not just in the photograph album. Your memories are in one another. There are many things you can do that could help to keep the spirit of your wedding day growing and deepening. May I suggest two simple ways?

Make sure you continue to take time out for one another. 'But of course we will – aren't we married?' Yes. But matters can creep up: pressure to do so many things; to pay for what you want or need; to make every moment 'productive'; to be successful. Take your wedding day as a kind of model. You took the time out, not earning money; but it may be one of the most productive days of your life, in terms of quality of true life. You celebrated what is beautiful and sacred. You had music (did you sing?). You lit candles. You told stories. You smiled a lot. All of this is 'making love'. There are times when things need to be done. But there are times when we need to 'do' nothing, just be. Just to be, and to be alive, is holy. A time to let yourselves be renewed. This, by the way, is what we call 'Sabbath'. To rest, to stop doing. Remember to keep your Sabbath holy, and your Sabbath will keep you.

Make sure you have time to have a meal together. On your wedding day, you had a meal, together, with your friends. Was it good? We usually do this on special occasions like Christmas, birthdays, etc. There's something about sharing a meal together that unites people. It's a natural human experience. It would be hard to sit down at a table for a meal with someone you're not at peace with. If you can sit down together for a meal most days, you are blessed. If work or other factors seem to prevent it, can you plan that you can do it even just once a week. (Without the television!) Talk about the things that make up your lives. It's a strange experience if you're in a busy cafeteria, and you find yourself sharing a table with a stranger, and you don't talk: somehow, it doesn't seem natural. There's something holy about sharing food, and talking together. Does this remind you of something? Something we call 'Eucharist': sharing of food, with gratitude in our hearts, so we can grow more united in love. May this be your experience around your own table.

SUGGESTIONS FOR PRAYER TOGETHER

There are as many ways of praying as there are people! If you go to any good religious bookstore, you'll find more prayers in books than you could ever make use of. The suggestions that follow are simply that: suggestions. All the words we use, of course, are words developed by people over the centuries; but when you speak to each other as man and woman, as husband and wife, although you use these words, you do not normally use speeches composed by others. Sometimes you may quote a bit of a poem or book or song, but that is the exception.

It can be the same when we pray: praying from our hearts in our own words is the *normal* way to pray. You may say *'But I wouldn't know what words to use!'* When you speak normally to another person you do not usually plan beforehand what exact words you will use, unless you're in an unusual situation like giving a speech where you have to have every word planned; you simply know what you want to say, and you say it, hardly noticing the words at all! If there's something in your heart or mind that you want to say, you can say it in prayer as well – no matter if you don't use the kind of 'holy language' we sometimes associate with prayer.

A person may say 'But when I'm speaking to another person, usually he or she is speaking back to me; it's very hard to hold a one-sided conversation!' That's true. So how do you listen to the 'other side' of the conversation in prayer? Thinking of a 'conversation' with God, how does he speak to us? You may already have your own experience of this; I'd like just to offer a few ideas.

It is the exception for us to hear the voice of God calling out our human language direct from heaven. He speaks to us in the everyday happenings of life, and in the words of scripture which we call the Bible, and in the persons of those around us. How does this work?

Take a few minutes to think over how yesterday and today were for you: the good feelings you had at times, and the bad feelings, and the times when you didn't seem to feel anything much at all. If you can, write down what you were doing right through the day. Now; if it is true, as we say, that God has us always in his care, is there some way you can see that care shown during the day? If so, take whatever that way was as God's way of saying 'I love you'; tell him in your own words how it was for you: how it was you felt; and what difference it makes to you now as you think of it. Then wait a minute just in silence, not trying to say a word. (Don't you often have 'good silences' with a person who loves you?)

Is there some way you can see that you didn't in the least feel cared for – perhaps quite the opposite? Again, tell him in your own words how it was for you – even how hurt, or angry, or lonely, or whatever you felt; and say something like 'What on earth were you doing there? What were you trying to teach me? Was that a way to help me become a more loving or patient or forgiving or peaceable person?' Then wait a minute in silence again, not even trying to say a word, but letting the experience sink in. Then continue, whenever you feel you want to.

I think it's some way like this that prayer starts for many people, both today and in biblical times. In the happenings of everyday life, ordinary or extraordinary, and in the encounter with the people who touch our lives, we learn to recognise the touch of God. It can just grow from there, if we give it a chance. In fact, many people already pray like that, without being aware of it; or if they are aware of it, they sometimes think 'But that's not *real* prayer.' What could be more real?

If it goes dry on you: that's normal. You don't speak or act now quite the way you used to ten years ago – if you're alive at all, you're continually changing, though you may not notice it at the time. It would be strange if your prayer was the same now as it was ten years ago, or as it will be ten years from now. If the well runs dry, it could be because you are simply not genuine about your relationship with God; if it's real, it must make a difference to your life. It could also be that there is something wrong in your way of life that is blocking the relationship. But if you are genuine about it, and if you are not aware of anything wrong in your way of life, then it may simply be a sign that you are going beyond this level of your relationship into a deeper level. Reflect and pray about that very experience of dryness; share it with someone who loves you and who will listen; and leave God to bring you on when he knows you're ready.

It can be helped to grow by sharing it with one another: how your partner reflects on the touch of God may be a way you never thought of; and your way may be a revelation to him or her!

It can, of course, be necessary at times to use set forms of prayer, especially when we are in a group for formal worship like Mass; it can also be helpful to be able to use the words of someone else for our prayers, particularly when we feel that we cannot find words of our own to pray. But we will feel much more at home with that kind of prayer if we normally can turn to God in our own personal way. Without our own prayer, the other can be simply tedious or artificial, or impossible.

So I encourage you to share whatever your own prayer already is with each other – no matter what it may be. And try to take the following suggestions as being from other people wanting to share their experience of prayer with you, so that you can grow through that. Change them any way you want to: it's *your* prayer that matters here.

There's a Bible full of riches for you to use!

1: Alone Together
For the first time after the Wedding!

(See the prayer of Tobias and Sarah on the evening of their wedding day; Tobit 8:4-8)

> You are blessed, God of our Fathers.
> Blessed, too, is your name for ever and ever.
> Let the heavens bless you
> and all things you have made, for evermore.
> It was you who said
> 'It is not good that man should be alone.'
> And so we do not take one another for any lustful motives;
> we do it in sincerity of heart.
> Be kind enough to have mercy on us
> and bring us to old age together.
> Amen! Amen!

Almighty God, so much has happened today.
Thank you for it all:
both what we liked and what we found difficult.
Thank you for all the people, too,
and for those who sent greetings and gifts.
You know exactly how we both feel.
Grant us now a new gentleness and tenderness
as we give ourselves to each other in love
for the first time as husband and wife.
May your gift of love heal our anxieties and hurts.
Help us to learn together how to put love into practice.
May our life together give praise to you;
for the kingdom, the power and the glory are yours
now and forever.
Amen!

Scripture Reflection

'The Song of Songs' (also called the 'Song of Solomon', or the 'Canticle of Canticles' – a collection of songs in the Bible celebrating the love of one person for another; or any of the scripture readings suggested for weddings.

2: After the Honeymoon, Setting up Home

(See the prayer of Solomon, when the temple was ready: 1 Kings 8:15, 27, 28)

> Blessed be the Lord, the God of Israel!
> The heavens, and their heavens, cannot contain you!
> – how much less this house!
> Listen to the prayer your servants make to you today.
> Day and night let your eyes watch over this house,
> over this place of which you have said
> 'My name shall be there'.

Blessed are you, Lord God of our marriage!
We thank you for your promise to be always faithful to us.
Be close to us, and keep us close to you and to each other.
May this home remind us, and all who come here, of your love.
When we have difficulties with each other, or with others,
remind us that love is always patient and kind;
love is never jealous, boastful, or conceited;
love is always ready to excuse, to trust, to hope,
and to endure whatever comes.
Show us how we can play our active part
in our home, our parish, and our neighbourhood.
We want to praise you here at home
and with our fellow Christians
and everywhere we go;

for the kingdom, the power, and the glory are yours
now and forever.
Amen!

Scripture Reflection

1 Corinthians 13; Galatians 5:13-25.

3: During the First Year of Marriage

(See the Song of Zechariah, Luke 1:68-79.)

Blessed be the Lord, the God of Israel;
he has come to his people and set them free.
He has raised up for us a mighty saviour.
In the tender compassion of our God,
the dawn from on high shall break upon us,
to shine on those who dwell in darkness
and the shadow of death,
and to guide our feet on the road of peace.

Blessed are you, O Lord our God, king of the universe:
we bless you each day of our married life.
Renew your blessing within us
as we choose each day, by your grace,
to be a living sign of your eternal love.
May we come to know, love, accept,
forgive, and encourage each other anew.
We ask you to guide us today as...
(either or both of you could mention whatever situation seems important),
for the kingdom, the power, and the glory are yours
now and forever.
Amen!

Scripture Reflection
1 John 4:7-12; or any of the Scripture readings suggested for weddings.

4: Home Blessing for the Lord's Day

The celebration of the Lord's Day starts on the evening of Saturday.
We celebrate the coming of the first day of the week:
the day of the creation of light (Genesis 1:1-5);
the day of the resurrection of Jesus (Luke 24:1-8);
the day of the coming of the Spirit (Acts 2:1-47);
the day of the gathering of the Christian community to celebrate the presence of the risen Jesus among the people gathered in his name (Matthew 18:20), in the proclamation of the word of Scripture (Luke 24:25-32), and in the breaking of the bread of life (Luke 24:33-35).

At the start of the Saturday evening meal, or at another suitable time, one person may light a candle as a sign of all this; another person may pray the following prayer, or another similar prayer, aloud:

Blessed are you, O Lord our God,
our Father, king of the universe:
you created light in order to scatter the darkness of the world.
You raised Jesus, the light of the world
in order to scatter the darkness of our lives.
You fill us with the Spirit of Jesus
so that we may live by his light.
We bless your holy name as we kindle this light,
(light the candle now)
one of our many gifts to us.
Rekindle, we pray, the flame of the Holy Spirit
as we praise you for this Day of the Lord.

All: *Come, Lord Jesus!*

Come, Lord Jesus!
Come, Lord Jesus!

Scripture Reflection
One of the Scripture readings for Sunday Mass, or one of the readings referred to above, could now be read, and those present could share briefly some reflections on it, questions about it, and how you would respond to it in your own life.

5: Blessing of Bread

Bread may be blessed before sharing it – like Grace before meals. Bread in the Christian tradition is very much a sign of fellowship and unity. It may be blessed by the priest at the end of Mass; or it may be blessed by any Christian on any occasion. It may be normal, everyday bread, or it may be specially made – perhaps a festive cake! If possible, let it be 'one bread' – one loaf or cake – which is blessed, and which is then broken or cut. But you may also have many smaller pieces. Whichever way you start, let each person, on receiving a piece, break it in two and offer it to another person, and in turn receive a portion from still another. In Greece the blessed bread is known as *antidoron,* in France it is *pain bénit,* in Poland it is *oplatki.*

Here is a form of blessing which could be used or adapted. A short Scripture passage such as one of the following could be read first.

Jesus was led by the Spirit out into the wilderness to be tempted by the devil. He fasted for forty days and forty nights, after which he was very hungry, and the tempter came and said to him, 'If you are the Son of God, tell these stones to turn into loaves.' But he replied, 'Scripture says: man does not live on bread alone, but on every word that comes from the mouth of God.' *(Matthew 4:1-4)*

Jesus said, 'It is my Father who gives you the bread from heaven, the true bread; for the bread of God is that which comes down from heaven and gives life to the world.' 'Sir', they said, 'give us that bread always.' Jesus answered: 'I am the bread of life'. *(John 6:32-35)*

The faithful all lived together and owned everything in common; they sold their goods and possessions and shared out the proceeds among themselves according to what each one needed. They went as a body to the Temple every day but met in the houses for the breaking of bread; they shared their food gladly and generously. *(Acts 2:44-47)*

Blessed are you, Lord God of all creation!
Through your goodness we have this bread to share.
As it is formed of many grains gathered from many fields,
yet now united as one bread,
so may we who share it be satisfied in body
and united in mind and heart as one Body.
As it is the work of many hands,
may we who share it work together
to share with all the world
your gifts of food for body and soul
so that your kingdom may come.
As we draw strength from it for living in your love,
may it fill us with thanksgiving for all the food we receive today;
may it protect us from sickness and sin;
may it free us from greed and fill us with joy
so that we may bless your glorious name for ever and ever
through Christ, our Lord. Amen!

6: Prayer Together with the Good News Day by Day

Before the Good News

Everybody

In the name of the Father, and of the Son, and of the Holy Spirit. Amen.

Reader 1

Lord, you said: Wherever two or three are gathered together in my name, I am there among them. You are with us now. Make us aware of your presence.

Everybody

Help us to think and to pray.

Reader 2

Lord, we are here tonight to listen to your word. We are here to search for your truth.

Everybody

Help us to think and to pray.

Reader 3

Lord, in the noise and bustle of life, it is not easy to find your truth. Help us to be quiet and still. Make us attentive to you tonight. For you alone have the words of eternal life.

Everybody

Help us to think and to pray.

Reader 4

Lord, by sin and selfishness we have hardened our hearts.
Open our eyes to your truth.

Open our hearts to your love.
Help us to know life at its best.

Everybody
Help us to think and to pray.

Leader
Let us pray.

Everybody
God our Father, only you can give meaning and purpose to life. Let your truth sink deeply into our hearts for others.
We offer our prayer with Christ our Lord.
Amen.

The Good News – Read/Think/Talk/Pray

1. *One person reads slowly the passage of Scripture chosen for the day.*
2. *All think for a while about what has been read.*
3. *They talk together about the meaning of the reading for them.*
4. *They then pray as they feel moved and also mention their own intentions.*

At the End
Pray for forgiveness

Everybody
Lord, forgive us all the wrong we have done this day.
Forgive us if we have been bad-tempered and hard to live with.
Forgive us if we have hurt those we should love.
Forgive us if we have made life more difficult for anyone.
Forgive us if we did not speak a word of comfort or praise or thanks when we should have done so.
Forgive us if we did not help someone in need when we should have done so.
Pray for all people.

Everybody
Lord, we pray tonight for all men and women,
for the good and for the bad;
for the believer and for the unbeliever;
for those who are trying to find you, and for those who are trying to ignore you.

Bless those who are alone, and who feel their loneliness worst of all at evening time.

Bless those who are old, those who are sick, those who will not sleep tonight.

Bless all homes and families. Bless those who have no home of their own.

Give us all restful sleep, and the peace of heart that comes from knowing that our sins are forgiven, and that we are always in the hands of our heavenly Father.

Everybody
'Our Father'
'Hail Mary'

Leader
May the Lord bless us,
May he keep us from all harm and lead us to that final day when there will be a new heaven and a new earth, when God will be all in all. Amen.

There are many resource books available in religious bookstores with a wealth of suggestions for home prayer and customs throughout the year and for special occasions. Nobody can do them all; but it is good for each home to have some ways of expressing and sharing faith at home.

RENEWAL ON YOUR ANNIVERSARIES

There are many possible ways of celebrating a renewal of your marriage: there is no one 'official' form of ceremony. It could be a ceremony on its own, starting with some prayer taken from or adapted from the wedding ceremony itself, and with one or more Scripture readings; or it could be within the celebration of Mass. The ceremony could be arranged for an individual couple or for a number of couples together. It could be in your own home, or in a church or other meeting place. Perhaps your parish will have an annual celebration for married couples.

The following is offered simply as material that could be used or adapted. The first part is from 'Renewal of Marriage Vows' in **A Prayer Book For Holy Year** *(Talbot Press: Dublin, 1974); the form of consent and the prayer that follows are adapted from the wedding ceremony.*

All: Father,
Your son has shown us how to love,
and invites us to love one another
as he loves us. We confess that our lives
have not always been a fulfilment of this.
We have been proud and selfish,
impatient with each other,
too interested in ourselves.
We have not trusted enough in your love
and in the love of each other.
We have not always been open with each other,
afraid to take the chance
that in loving, we may not be loved in return.
There are times when we have had the opportunity
to make our love for one another a reality,
and we have remained silent.
Father,
forgive our unkind words,
our impatient gestures, our selfish deeds.

Forgive our failure
to become involved in the needs of others. *(Pause)*

P: Having confessed our sins let us make together a profession of love.

All married couples:
We believe that, by our love, we bear witness to the union of Christ and his Church.
We believe that we are meant to be for each other a sign of Christ's love.
We believe that we are called to bring one another to God.
We believe that we are called to give ourselves in service to God and humankind.
We believe that we are meant to help our children look beyond us and give themselves in service to God and humankind.
Believing these things, we offer ourselves, together, as husband and wife, to God, so that our love may become his love, through Christ our Lord. Amen.

Husband: N., do you renew your consent to be my wife?
Wife: I do.
N. do you renew your consent to be my husband?
Husband: I do.

(Join hands and say together:)
Both: We take each other again as husband and wife
and promise to love each other truly
for better, for worse,
for richer, for poorer,
in sickness and health,
till death do us part
(*or:* all the days of our life).

The couple say together the following or similar prayer:
We thank you Lord,
and we praise you
for bringing us
to this happy day.

You gave us to each other
... years ago.
Now, together, we give ourselves again to you.
We ask you, Lord:
continue making us one in our love;
continue keeping us one in your peace.

Protect our marriage.
Bless our home.
Make us gentle.
Keep us faithful.

And when life is over,
unite us again
where parting is no more
in the kingdom of your love.

There we will praise you
in the happiness and peace
of our eternal home.
Amen.

CONTACTS

The following is a small selection of sources you may wish to contact – it is by no means exhaustive. This information is correct at the time of writing (August 2002). Naturally, changes may occur with the passage of time, so, if you find the information is no longer correct, you may need to check elsewhere for up-to-date information. Your own parish is a good contact point for many sources of information.

For Marriage Preparation, ACCORD works in all parts of the country.

1. **ACCORD**
   Agency for the service of all aspects of marriage and family life, including marriage preparation, counselling, family planning, etc. Offices all around Ireland. Consult your local telephone directory, or check the website: *www.accord.ie*

2. **www.gettingmarried.ie** or
   www.catholicireland.net/gettingmarried
   A website to help you plan your wedding. There are many websites and computer programs for wedding planning, dealing with non-church things of a wedding day. This website deals with the rite of the Catholic Church in Ireland. Useful internet links to many other sites.

3. **The Association of Interchurch Families**
   For families where husband and wife belong to different Christian Churches or communions. This association can be contacted through the Irish School of Ecumenics, Bea House, Miltown Park, Dublin 6, Ireland or by sending e-mail to *kelisara@eircom.net*.
   Website: *http://luggage.connect.ie/~aif/*

4. **Marriage Encounter Ireland**
   For the enrichment and deepening of marriage. Website:

www.ireland.wwme.org or *www.marriageencounterireland.com* for up-to-date information. Des & Sue Milne at 01 8453517 or Fr Gregory Carroll OP at 01 8897630.

5. **NAOMI:**
   National Association of the Ovulation Method of Ireland
   Natural Family Planning. Contact them at 16 North Great George's Street, Dublin 1; or on their website: *www.naomi.ie*

6. **If pregnancy is a problem:**
   CURA: A Catholic agency, offering support for anyone, married or single, with a problem pregnancy. Offices around Ireland – see your local telephone book. Helpline: 1850 622 626. Website: *www.cura.ie*
   Life Ireland: an Irish organisation dedicated to counselling women with crisis pregnancies. Offices around Ireland. Helpline: 1850 281 281. 29/30. Dame Street, Dublin 2. Website: *www.life.ie*

7. **Wedding in Rome**
   Make sure to arrange well in advance.
   Irish College, Rome: Pontificio Collegio Irlandese, Via dei Santi Quattro 1, 00184 Roma, Italy. Website: *www.irishcollege.org*
   St Patrick's College, Rome (Augustinians): St Patrick's Church, Via Boncompagni 31, 00187 Roma, Italy. Website: *www.geocities.com/MotorCity/1197/weddings.html*

8. **Information on civil registration of marriage, marriage certificates, etc.**
   General Register Office for the Republic of Ireland: Registrar-General of Marriages, Joyce House, 8-11 Lombard Street East, Dublin 2. Tel. 01-635 40 00. Website: *www.groireland.ie/getting_married.htm*
   General Register Office, Northern Ireland: General Register Office (N.I), Oxford House, 49-55 Chister Street Belfast BT1 4HL; Tel. (08)(01232) 252 000. Website: *www.groni.gov.uk*

9. **INTAMS: International Academy for Marital Spirituality**
Foundation for the promotion of marriage and family pastoral ministry. Website: *www.intams.com*

APPENDICES

APPENDIX 1

IRISH LANGUAGE RITE IN ENGLISH TRANSLATION

See page 175 for the Rite in Irish

GAIRMGLAOCH – SOLEMN CALLING

P: Be mindful that we are gathered together here
on the … day of … in the year of the Lord …
to receive the marriage vows of N. and N.
to union and agreement;
to love and faithfulness;
to respect and honour;
to kindness and fairness;
to courage and celebration;
to oneness and forgiveness;
to nobility and dignity;
to steadfastness till death.

In the presence of God and his Church,
in the name of the most Holy Trinity,
and in the peace we have from the Passion of Christ;

in honour of the Virgin Mary, the mother of God,
of the holy Apostles and of all the saints;
in the power of the Blessed Sacrament:
I ask you solemnly if you are willing
to accept each other as husband and wife?

Couple: We are willing.

P: Will you accept any children God may send you, and will you bring them up in accordance with the law of Christ and of his Church?

Couple: We will accept them, and we will bring them up in this way.

DEARBH TOILEANAIS – EXCHANGE OF CONSENT

Minister: I invite you to declare before God and his Church your consent to become husband and wife.

(Bride and bridegroom join hands.)

Groom: I, N., take you N., as my wife,
for better, for worse,
for richer, for poorer,
in sickness and in health,
till death do us part. *(Or:* all the days of our life.*)*

Bride: I, N., take you N., as my husband,
for better, for worse,
for richer, for poorer,
in sickness and in health,
till death do us part. *(Or:* all the days of our life.*)*

Minister: What God joins together, no person may separate.
May God strengthen the decision you have given one another, and may he grant you his blessing generously.

Beann na bhFáinní – Blessing of Rings

Minister: Lord, bless N. and N., and consecrate their married life.
May this ring (these rings) be a symbol of their faithfulness,
and a reminder of their love for one another.
This is our prayer through Christ our Lord.

People: Amen.

The bridegroom places a ring on the bride's finger; he may say:

N., wear this ring as a sign of our faithful love.
In the name of the Father, and of the Son, and of the Holy Spirit.

The bride may place a ring on the bridegroom's finger; she may say:

N., wear this ring as a sign of our faithful love.
In the name of the Father, and of the Son, and of the Holy Spirit.

An Tabhartas – The Gift

The bridegroom may give a small symbolic gift to the bride; or each may give the other a small symbolic gift; they may say:

I give you this gold/silver/gift, as a token of all I possess.

Guí an Phobail – Prayer of the Faithful

P: Let us pray.
At the wedding in Cana, the very King of All Grace was there in person. Let us ask him to bless this couple, as he blessed that celebration in Galilee.

B: Jesus, son of Mary,
have mercy on us.

People: You are King of Kings
and God of all creation.

G: Be at the start of our way
and at the end of our living.

People: You are King of Kings
and God of all creation.

B: Be at the awakening of our life
and at the darkening of our day.

People: You are King of Kings
and God of all creation.

G: Go before us and with us
to the end of our undertaking.

People: You are King of Kings
and God of all creation.

B: Make us holy
in our living and in our growing.

People: You are King of Kings
and God of all creation.

G: Make us holy
in all we are and have.

People: You are King of Kings
and God of all creation.

B: Make us holy
in our loving and in our believing.

People: You are King of Kings
and God of all creation.

G: Our loving and our believing
each day is for you.

People: You are King of Kings
and God of all creation.

Father of Bride:
May you be blessed in prosperity,
Blessed in sons and daughters,
Blessed on land and sea.

Mother of Bride:

May you be blessed in your love,
Blessed in your faithfulness,
Blessed by heavenly kingdom,
Blessed by day and night.

Father of Groom:

May the goodness of the sea be yours,
the goodness of the land be yours,
the goodness of heaven be yours.

Mother of Groom:

May each day bring you happiness,
And no day leave you worse;
May you be honoured and respected,
And have the love of each person you meet.

Priest: Eternal God,
in your almighty power,
look down on your servants N. and N.,
who are now united in marriage here today.
Grant them, for the sake of their love for each other,
that they may be constant in your love.
We ask this through Christ our Lord.

People: Amen.

Beannú an Phósta

(See page 208 for the Rite)

Nuptial Blessing

The couple kneels before the altar.

P: Let us ask God to send his blessing on N.
and N. and unite them in love.

All pray silently for a while.

God our Father, you created the universe.
You made a human person from the soil of the earth
and into the nostrils you blew the breath of life,
thus making a living being.
And you said: It is not good that this person be alone;
I will made a worthy helpmate to match.
And, causing a deep sleep to fall on him,
You took a rib and covered it in flesh.
This you made into woman,
and brought her to the man, who said:
This at last is bone of my bone and flesh of my flesh!
She shall be called woman
because she was called into being from man.
For this reason, a man leaves father and mother
and holds fast to his wife
and they come to be one flesh.
You blessed them and said
Be fruitful and multiply
and fill the earth and subdue it.
Therefore, Lord God,
grant your generous blessing
to your servants here, N. and N.
Bless them as you blessed
Abraham and Sarah,
Isaac and Rebecca,
Zachary and Elizabeth,
Joachim and Anne.
Protect them, Lord,
as you protected Noah from the flood,
The three in the fiery furnace,
Isaac from the sword,
and the people of Moses from slavery in Egypt.

Look kindly on N.
May she live in peace with you
and follow the example of those women
who are praised in the Scriptures.
May she have the cheerfulness of Rachel
and the wisdom of Rebecca
and a long life of faithfulness like Sarah.
May she be blessed in her looks and in her speech.
May she be blessed in her health and in her beauty.
May she be blessed in love and in grace.

May N. put his trust in her,
and may she be a companion to him.
May he always esteem her and love her
as Christ does the Church.

Father,
keep this couple strong in faith
and true to your commands.
May they be faithful to each other,
examples of Christian living,
and witnesses to Christ.
May they see their children's children.
And after a long and happy life together,
May they find joy in the company of your saints in heaven.
We ask this through Christ, our Lord.

People: Amen.

BEANNACHT AG DEIREADH AN AIFRINN

(See page 215 for the Rite)

Final Blessing

The priest holds a Cross of St Brigid in his right hand throughout the blessing. With it, he makes the sign of the cross over the couple and over the people. Then he gives the cross to the bride (or to the couple), who put it up on the wall of their home each St Brigid's Day throughout their married life.

P:	The peace of the Father be with you. The peace of Christ be with you. The peace of the Spirit be with you Every day and every night. Amen.
People:	Every day and night. Amen.
P:	May the Father protect you. May Christ protect you. May the Spirit protect you Every day and night of your life. Amen.
People:	Every day and night of your life. Amen.
P:	The blessing of the Father come upon you. The blessing of Christ come upon you. The blessing of the Spirit come upon you Until you are crowned with eternal life. Amen.
People:	Until you are crowned with eternal life. Amen.
P:	May God prosper you from Samhain to St Brigid's Day to May Day, from May Day to Lúnasa, and from Lúnasa to Samhain, and may almighty God bless you: Father, Son, and Holy Spirit.
People:	Amen.
P:	Go now, safe in the peace of Christ.
People:	Thanks be to God.

APPENDIX 2

SAMPLE ALTERNATIVE ADDRESS AT WEDDING RITE

On page 168 there are three suggested forms of Address and Questions to the Couple. However, it may also be in 'similar words'; you may devise your own, as long as it has the same essential content. The following is a sample of how this might be done by a couple and minister who wish to give the couple a more prominent part to play. It is based in part on the third suggested form, with some additions. Shorter versions of a format such as this could, of course, be devised.

The first section of what follows could take place after the opening greeting, and the second section after the homily; or all could take place after the homily.

Minister: N. and N., with what purpose in mind have you come here today?

Couple: We have come here to pledge our love before God and before the Church assembled here; in becoming husband and wife, we give ourselves to each other for life.

Minister: What do you intend by this?

Couple: We promise to be true and faithful, to support and cherish each other until death, so that our years together will be the living out in love of the pledge we now make. We pray, and we ask you to pray, that our love for each other may reflect the enduring love of Christ for his Church.

Minister: Do you accept that your marriage will be a sacrament: a sign and instrument of the grace and love of God all your life long?

Couple: We do.
As we face the future together, we want to keep in mind that the sacrament of marriage unites us with Christ, and brings us, through the years, the grace and blessing of God our Father.

Minister: How will you carry out your intention?

Couple: Marriage is from God: he alone can give us the happiness that goes beyond human expectation, and that grows deeper through the difficulties and struggles of life. We will put our trust in God as we set out together in life.

Minister: How will this be seen in your home?

Couple: We will make our home a centre of Christian family life. [*In this, we dearly want to bequeath to any children God may give us a heritage more lasting than all the wealth of this world.]
We believe firmly that a Christian home makes Christ and his Church present in the world of everyday things. We pray that all who will enter our home may find there the presence of the Lord; for he has said: 'Where two or three are gathered together in my name, there am I in the midst of them.'

Minister: I now turn to all those assemble here, and I ask you: Do you accept that you share with N. and N. responsibility for their future, and do you pledge your support, your love, and your blessing to them in this life you are beginning?

Guests: From our hearts, we do!

Minister: Will you, by God's grace, pledge to do everything in your power to uphold and care for these two people in their life together?

Guests: We will!

(If the above takes place at the start of the celebration, for example after the opening greeting of the Wedding Mass, it could conclude here, and be followed by the Penitential Rite: For example:
'We know that we who follow Christ will not live a life of love, unless we know God's forgiveness, and unless we forgive, and ask forgiveness of, one another. Let us therefore now call to mind our sins.' Then the final section would follow the homily.)

Minister: N. and N., as you are about to exchange your marriage vows, the Church wishes to be assured that you appreciate the meaning of what you do, and so I ask you:
Have you come here of your own free will and choice and without compulsion to marry each other?

Couple: We have.

Minister: Will you love and honour each other in marriage all the days of your life?

Couple: We will.

[**Minister:* Are you willing to accept with love the children God may send you, and bring them up in accordance with the law of Christ and his Church?

Couple: We are.]

The rite now continues with the invitation to declare consent: p. 170.

The parts above marked [...] may be omitted in particular cases – for example, if the couple are advanced in years.*

APPENDIX 3

RITES FOR SCOTLAND, ENGLAND AND WALES

RITE FOR SCOTLAND

All stand, including the bride and bridegroom, and the priest addresses them in these or similar words:

P: N. and N. *(Christian names)*, you have come together in this church so that the Lord may seal and strengthen your love. Christ abundantly blesses this love. He has already consecrated you by baptism and now he enriches and strengthens you by a special sacrament, so that you may assume the duties of marriage in mutual and lasting fidelity. And so, in the presence of the Church – before me, its minister, and with these your friends as witnesses – I ask you to state your intentions to live in lifelong fidelity to each other and to God in whose image you have been made.

The priest then questions them about their freedom of choice, faithfulness to each other and the acceptance and upbringing of children.

P: I now ask you if you undertake the obligations of marriage, freely and deliberately. N. and N., are you ready, freely and without reservation, to give yourselves to each other in marriage?

Each answers separately, first the bridegroom, then the bride:

G: I am.
B: I am.
P: Will you love and honour each other as man and wife, for the rest of your lives?
G: I will.
B: I will.

The following question may be omitted if, for example, the couple is advanced in years:

P: Will you accept children lovingly from God and bring them up according to the law of Christ and his Church?
G: I will.
B: I will.

The Consent

(At an appropriate part of the ceremony, according to local custom, the bride may be 'given away' by a relative or close friend.)

The priest invites the bride and bridegroom to declare their consent.

P: Since it is your intention to enter into marriage, declare your consent before God and his Church.

First he asks the bridegroom, inserting the full names:

P: N. N., do you freely and willingly take N. N., here present, for your lawful wife according to the laws of God and of Holy Mother Church?

G: I do.

Then he asks the bride, inserting the full names:

P: N. N., do you freely and willingly take N. N., here present, for your lawful husband according to the laws of God and of Holy Mother Church?

B: I do.

The priest then says to the bridegroom and bride:

P: N. and N., join your right hands.

The bridegroom takes the bride's right hand in his and says (or repeats after the priest):

G: I, N.N.,
take you, N. N.,
for my lawful wife,
to have and to hold
from this day forward:
for better, for worse;
for richer; for poorer;
in sickness and in health
till death do us part.

The bride says (or repeats after the priest):

B: I, N. N.,
take you, N. N.,
for my lawful husband,
to have and to hold

from this day forward:
for better, for worse;
for richer, for poorer;
in sickness and in health
till death do us part.

Having received their consent, the priest says:

P: You have declared your consent before the Church.
May the Lord in his goodness strengthen your married love.

Then the priest declares to all present:

P 'What God has joined together, let no man put asunder.'
(Matthew 19:6)

All present reply:

Amen.

And the couple release their hands.

Blessing and Exchange of the Ring or Rings

The priest blesses the ring or rings, handed to him by the best man or a server.

P: May the Lord bless this ring (or rings), which you give (to each other) as the sign of your love and fidelity.
All: Amen.

or 2

P: Lord, bless and consecrate N. and N. *(Christian names)* in their love for each other. May this ring (these rings) be a symbol of true faith in each other and always remind them of their love. (Grant this) through Christ our Lord.

All: Amen.

or 3 (only when two rings are to be blessed):

P: Lord, bless these rings which we bless in your name. Grant that those who wear them may always have a deep faith in each other. May they do your will and always live together in peace, good will and love. (We ask this) through Christ our Lord.

All: Amen.

He may sprinkle the ring or rings with holy water.

The bridegroom gives the ring to his bride, putting it on the fourth finger of her left hand, saying:

G: With this ring I wed you,
in the name of the Father
and of the Son
and of the Holy Spirit.
Amen.

The bridegroom may also hand (gold and) silver to his bride, saying:

G: This (gold and) silver I give you,
token (tokens) of all my worldly goods.

If the bride gives a ring to her bridegroom, she does so in the same manner, saying:

B. With this ring I wed you,
in the name of the Father
and of the Son

and of the Holy Spirit.
Amen.

RITE FOR ENGLAND AND WALES

The priest speaks to the bride and bridegroom in these or similar words:

Address

P. N. and N. *(Christian names only)*, you have come together in this church so that the Lord may seal and strengthen your love in the presence of the Church's minister and this community. Christ abundantly blesses this love. He has already consecrated you in baptism and now he enriches and strengthens you by a special sacrament so that you may assume the duties of marriage in mutual and lasting fidelity. And so, in the presence of the Church, I ask you to state your intentions.

The Questions

P: N. and N. *(Christian names only)*, I shall now ask you if you freely undertake the obligations of marriage, and to state that there is no legal impediment to your marriage.

The priest puts each question once only, but bride and bridegroom answer separately:

Are you ready, freely and without reservation, to give yourselves to each other in marriage?

G: I am.

B: I am.

P: Are you ready to love and honour each other as man and wife for the rest of your lives?

G: I am.

B: I am.

The priest may omit the next question if, for example, the couple are advanced in years.

[*P: Are you ready to accept children lovingly from God and bring them up according to the Law of Christ and his Church?

G: I am.

B: I am.]

The next words of the bridegroom and the bride are necessary for the civil validity of the marriage. They may either read or say them after the priest.

G: I do solemnly declare
that I know not
of any lawful impediment
why I, N. N. *(full name, including surname),*
may not be joined in matrimony to N. N. *(bride's full name, including surname).*

B: I do solemnly declare
that I know not
of any lawful impediment
why I, N. N. *(full name, including surname),*
may not be joined in matrimony to N. N. *(bridegroom's full name, including surname).*

Declaration of Consent

P: Since it is your intention to enter into marriage, declare your consent before God and his Church.

To the Bridegroom:

N. N., will you take N. N., here present, for your lawful wife, according to the rite of our Holy Mother, the Church?

G: I will.

To the Bride:

N. N., will you take N. N., here present, for your lawful husband, according to the rite of our Holy Mother, the Church?

B: I will.

The bride and bridgroom join their right hands. The bride's hand may be placed in the bridegroom's by the man who gives her away. The next words of the bridegroom and the bride are necessary for the civil validity of the marriage. They may either read them or say them after the priest.

G: I call upon these persons here present to witness
that I, N. N. *(full name, including surname)*,
do take thee, N. N. *(full name, including surname)*
to be my lawful wedded wife,
to have and to hold from this day forward,
for better, for worse,
for richer, for poorer,
in sickness and in health,
to love and to cherish,
till death do us part.

They separate their hands for a moment and then rejoin them.

B: I call upon these persons here present to witness
that I, N. N. *(full name, including surname)*,
do take thee, N. N. *(full name, including surname)*
to be my lawful wedded husband,
to have and to hold from this day forward,
for better, for worse,
for richer, for poorer,

in sickness and in health,
to love and to cherish,
till death do us part.

P: You have declared your consent before the Church. May the Lord in his goodness strengthen your consent and fill you both with his blessings. What God has joined together, let no man put asunder.

All: Amen.

Blessing of Rings

The priest blesses the ring or rings

P: May the Lord bless ✠ this ring (these rings) which you give (to each other) as the sign of your love and fidelity.

All: Amen.

The bridegroom places the ring on the bride's finger, saying,

G: N. *(Christian name only)*, take this ring as a sign of my love and fidelity. In the name of the Father, and of the Son, and of the Holy Spirit.

If the bride is giving the bridegroom a ring, she places it on his finger, saying,

B: N. *(Christian name only)*, take this ring as a sign of my love and fidelity. In the name of the Father, and of the Son, and of the Holy Spirit.

(Please consult your priest about the alternative formula for the Blessing of Rings.)

The Nuptial Blessing
(Scotland, England & Wales)

A choice of three forms:

1

After the Lord's Prayer, the prayer 'Deliver Us' is omitted. The priest faces the bride and bridegroom and says the following blessing over them. (If one or both of the parties will not be receiving Communion, the words in the introduction to the nuptial blessing, 'through the sacrament of the body and blood of Christ', may be omitted.

*If desired, in the prayer 'Father, by your power', two of the first three paragraphs may be omitted, keeping only the paragraph that corresponds to the reading of the Mass. In the last paragraph of this prayer, the words in brackets may be omitted whenever circumstances suggest it, for example if the couple is advanced in years**.)*

With hands joined, the priest says:

My dear friends, let us turn to the Lord and pray
that he will bless with his grace this woman (or N.)
now married in Christ to this man (or N.)
and that (through the sacrament of the body and blood of Christ,)
he will unite in love the couple he has joined in this holy bond.
All pray silently for a short while. Then the priest extends his hands and continues:

Father,
by your power you have made everything out of nothing.
In the beginning you created the universe
and made mankind in your own likeness.
You gave man the constant help of woman
so that man and woman should no longer be two, but one flesh,
and you teach us that what you have united
may never be divided.

Father,
by your plan man and woman are united,
and married life has been established
as the one blessing that was not forfeited by original sin
or washed away in the flood.
Look with love upon this woman, your daughter,
now joined to her husband in marriage.
She asks your blessing.
Give her the grace of love and peace.
May she always follow the example of the holy women
whose praises are sung in the scriptures.
May her husband put his trust in her
and recognise that she is his equal
and the heir with him to the life of grace.
May he always honour her and love her
as Christ loves his bride, the Church.
Father,
keep them always true to your commandments.
Keep them faithful in marriage
and let them be living examples of Christian life.

Give them the strength which comes from the gospel
so that they may be witnesses of Christ to others.
[Bless them with children
and help them to be good parents.
May they live to see their children's children.*]
And, after a happy old age,
grant them fullness of life with the saints
in the kingdom of heaven.

We ask this through Christ our Lord.

2

After the Lord's Prayer, the prayer 'Deliver Us' is omitted. The priest faces the bride and bridegroom and says the following blessing over them.

(In the prayer 'Holy Father', the paragraph, 'Holy Father, you created mankind', may be omitted, keeping only the paragraph that corresponds to the reading of the Mass.)

With hands joined, the priest says:

Let us pray to the Lord for N. and N.
who come to God's altar at the beginning of their married life
(as now they share in the body and blood of Christ).

All pray silently for a short while. Then the priest extends his hands and continues:

Holy Father,
you created mankind in your image
and made man and woman to be joined as husband and wife
in union of body and heart
and so fulfil their mission to the world.
Father,
to reveal the plan of your love,
you made the union of husband and wife
an image of the covenant between you and your people.
In the fulfilment of this sacrament,
the marriage of Christian man and woman
is a sign of the marriage between Christ and the Church.
Father, stretch out your hand, and bless N. and N.

Lord,
grant that as they begin to live this sacrament
they may share with each other the gifts of your love
and become one in heart and mind
as witnesses to your presence in their marriage.

Help them to create a home together
[and give them children to be formed by the gospel
and to have a place in your family.*]
Give your blessings to N., your daughter,
so that she may be a good wife [and mother*],
caring for the home,
faithful to her husband,
generous and kind.
Give your blessings to N., your son,
sot that he may be a faithful husband
[and a good father*].

The following sentence is added when both parties ask to receive Communion:

Father,
grant that as they come together to your table on earth,
so they may one day have the joy
of sharing your feast in heaven.

We ask this through Christ our Lord.

3

After the Lord's Prayer, the prayer 'Deliver Us' is omitted. The priest faces the bride and bridegroom and says the following blessing over them:

My dear friends, let us ask God
for his continued blessings upon this bridegroom and his bride (or N. and N.).

All pray silently for a short while. Then the priest extends his hands and continues:

Holy Father,
creator of the universe,

maker of man and woman in your own likeness,
source of blessing for married life,
we humbly pray to you for this woman
who today is united with her husband in this sacrament of marriage.
May your fullest blessing come upon her and her husband so that they may together rejoice in your gift of married love [and enrich your Church with their children*].

Lord,
may they both praise you when they are happy
and turn to you in their sorrows.
May they be glad that you help them in their work
and know that you are with them in their need.
May they pray to you in the community of the Church,
and be your witnesses in the world.
May they reach old age in the company of their friends,
and come at last to the kingdom of heaven.

We ask this through Christ our Lord.

The Solemn Blessing

(Scotland, England & Wales)

1

P: God the eternal Father keep you in love for each other,
so that the peace of Christ may stay with you
and be always in your home.
All: Amen.

P: May [your children bless you,*]
your friends console you
and all people live in peace with you.
All: Amen.

P: May you always bear witness to the love of God in this world
so that the afflicted and the needy
will find in you generous friends
and welcome you into the joys of heaven.

All: Amen.

P: May almighty God bless you,
the Father, ✠ and the Son, and the Holy Spirit.

All: Amen.

2

P: May God, the almighty Father,
give you his joy
and bless you [in your children*].

All: Amen.

P: May the only Son of God have mercy on you
and help you in good times and in bad.

All: Amen.

P: May the Holy Spirit of God
always fill your hearts with his love.

All: Amen.

P: And may almighty God bless you,
the Father, ✠ and the Son, and the Holy Spirit.

All: Amen.

3

P: May the Lord Jesus, who was a guest at the wedding at Cana,
bless you and your families and friends.

All: Amen.

P: May Jesus, who loved his Church to the end,
always fill your hearts with his love.

All: Amen.

P: May he grant that, as you believe in his resurrection,
so you may wait for him in joy and hope.

All: Amen.

P: And may almighty God bless you,
the Father, ✠ and the Son, and the Holy Spirit.

All: Amen.

APPENDIX 4

INTRODUCING THE BIBLE

Think of some newspaper or magazine you read. Now, imagine that you have in your hands not just one copy, but all the copies for a year. Would you start to read at the first page of the first issue, and keep going till you had read to the end of the last issue? You'd be most unusual to do that; you'd probably become fed up with the whole thing pretty quickly!

A different way would be to flick through, and pick out the parts that interest you; pieces that you might enjoy; that might help you in some way; parts that make sense to you. Doing that, you might notice another article or section you hadn't thought of at first, but you realise now is of interest. And so you get into it more.

In some ways, the Bible is like that. It's a collection of writings *(we usually call them 'books', though some are very short)*. It's like a small library of books, written over a long period of time. They are gathered together into one book that we usually call 'The Bible'. Many parts started long before they were ever written down. They were stories and memories passed on faithfully by word of mouth. Just pick the part you'd like to start with.

But I don't know anything about the Bible!
You may be surprised how much you know. If you go to church regularly, or even occasionally, you'll already be familiar with quite a bit.

Why bother reading stories of long ago?
For the same reason you like to read human-interest stories of today; or watch a film of *Robin Hood*; or follow the adventures of *Star Trek*: people trying to live their lives, facing difficulties, getting into a terrible mess sometimes; and sometimes discovering something tremendous. It's that 'something tremendous' that makes the Bible different.

Why do they use old-fashioned language?
Some Bibles do; but they don't have to. Words change as the years pass. Think of the number of words we use now that were not there thirty or forty years ago – or even less: *ecology; microwave; BSE; internet.* Or words, like *deadly, cool, politically correct, inclusive language,* which were and are used, but sometimes with quite a different meaning! You can probably think of others yourself.

You can get a Bible in old-fashioned language, if you feel better with it; or you can get one in more up-to-date language.

Why are Bibles different?

1. Because they were not written in languages we speak in Ireland today. They need to be translated from Hebrew and Greek. If someone says to you in Irish *'Conas tá tú?'*, you could translate that as *'How art thou?'*, or *'How are you?*; or as *'How do you do?'*; or, more casually, *'How's it going?'*; or many other ways. So you can look for a Bible that speaks to you in the way that you're more at home with. Mostly, the words will mean much the same; sometimes you'll notice differences of meaning.
2. Not all Christians agree on how important various writings are. We do agree on most parts. Some parts accepted by Roman Catholics are not accepted by some other Christians as being on

the same level as the rest. They are often called the '*Apocrypha*' or the '*Deuterocanonical Books*'. Some Bibles include these; some do not. You needn't let this put you off!

3. Some Bibles include notes to explain the meaning and background. Some notes are very full, some are very short, and some Bibles have no notes.
4. Some have large print and lots of pictures and are heavy to carry; others are smaller and lighter. You can get a full Bible or a part. The full Bible will have the parts written before the time of Jesus, usually called '*The Old Testament*' or '*The Jewish Scriptures*' (remember, Jesus and all his background are Jewish); and the parts written after the time of Jesus, usually called '*The New Testament*'. You can also get either part separately; or just one booklet containing one of the four Gospels telling the life of Jesus.

What are all those strange numbers and letters?

They are there to help you find your way; like knowing the meaning of road signs when you're driving. You should find a page at the start of the Bible, giving a list of the names of the books in it, with the page numbers for that Bible. Sometimes it will also give a shorter form. For example, for the book called '*Genesis*' (usually the first book), it may give the shorter form '*Gen*'; for '*Matthew*', it may also give '*Matt*' or '*Mt*'. You'll find that easy enough.

What if a friend of yours tells you about something worth reading in your Bible; but she or he has a different Bible with different page numbers? That's why, a long time ago, someone divided the books into *chapters*, and each chapter into smaller sections (like sentences) which we call '*Verses*'. Some short books only have verses. If you see '*Matthew 6:25-34*', it means St Matthew's Gospel, chapter 6, verses 25-34. This should mean pretty much the same no matter what Bible you look at. (Why not look for it now? You may think it's great, or that it's strange; but you'll have opened the Bible and found it!)

Sometimes there are two books with the same name. There are two books of Kings, and two letters to the Corinthians. It's still quite simple. If they do not spell it out, like *'The Second Book of Kings'*, you'll find a number *before* the name. Recognise *1 Corinthians 13:4-8?*

There are three letters of St John, as well as St John's Gospel. If you see a number before the name John, you'll know it's one of the letters. If there's no number before the name, it's the Gospel.

The book of Psalms has 150 songs/prayers called Psalms, not called 'chapters'; some long, some very short. Because of two different traditions of dividing them up, there can be a difference of one or two in the number of a particular Psalm. If you can't find what you want, look at the one or two before or after.

There's enough there to get you started. There are a few other things about these numbers. If you come across them, the Bible will usually have a note to explain.

Can I believe it all?

Yes: but not all in the same way.

Think of a newspaper. It has news reports, an editorial section, articles written by journalists and others, advertisements, cartoons. We don't read an advertisement as if it were an independent news report. Usually an advertisement that could seem to be a news report has to carry a warning that it is actually an advertisement. With an article commenting on some topic, it can be useful to know who the writer is, and what political background is involved. Sometimes a cartoon, even if it is completely fiction, may contain more truth than other items in the newspaper that may seem to be completely factual!

It's not as complicated as it may seem. Just because it's the Bible, we don't have to throw away the common sense that God gave us. We can use the same sort of judgement about what we read in the Bible as we normally do every day. If the Bible says that the sun rose, it does not mean that the sun really goes around the Earth. It means that that is the way that people spoke then (and now too); and we know what they mean. When the Gospels of Matthew, Mark, Luke and John speak of the Easter Sunday, the accounts don't agree in every way. They are accounts from different witnesses. What is clear is that they agree on this: Jesus is alive, and risen from the dead!

Is it not dangerous to read the Bible?

Well... Yes! But it's dangerous to have gas and electricity in the house. That doesn't usually prevent us having them. You may be surprised at the power (of a different kind) you find in the Bible.

Your local parish or church may have a group, so you're not alone. We can learn a lot by hearing how the Bible speaks to others. There may also be a group of people from different local churches: that can be especially enriching.

What if I meet problems?

It means that what you're reading is making some impression. There are parts of the Bible that are difficult to make sense of, like lists of names, and so on. And they had different customs at different times. As you get to know the Bible, you'll see that things change and develop. The fact that Abraham had more than one wife does not mean that we should do the same today. People may quote '*Eye for eye, tooth for tooth*' (Exodus 21:24), forgetting what Jesus said in Matthew 5:38-48. It's worth looking up. Words like his could lead someone to say: *The parts of the Bible I have most trouble with are not the parts I* ***don't*** *understand, but the parts I* ***do*** *understand!* Some parts of the Bible are very comforting and encouraging. Some offer a great challenge. Some will not seem to speak to you at the time; but that's okay too.

As you read, watch out for examples of the following kinds of writing. It can make it easier to understand them when you recognise them.

a. ***History:*** telling the story of the people of the time. It's never just history; it always tells of their relationship with God, and of their understanding of how God acts in their lives.

b. ***Wisdom:*** Wise sayings and advice for their time and situation. We need to ask for God's wisdom to apply these to our world in our own time and situation.

c. ***Prayer:*** Especially the Psalms, but also in many other parts of the Bible. Written for many different reasons. Many in heartfelt joy or anguish. Whatever your situation, you can often find a Psalm that will speak to you. Nearly every Christian recognises Psalm 23. (It may be 22 in your Bible: remember what we said above about Psalm numbers.)

d. ***Prophecy:*** This is not necessarily about telling the future. What it means first is: speaking the Word of God to the people of the day. The messenger is a spokesperson for God, whom we call a 'prophet'. The message can, of course, have a lot of meaning for people a long time afterwards.

e. ***Parables:*** The parables of Jesus are the most famous (you'll remember Luke 10:25-37). There are other similar stories in other parts of the Bible.

A Place to Start

1 ***You'll need a Bible.*** You may have one at home. If so, but if it's not one you realistically think you'd get started on, ask at your local church or at a bookshop. Prices vary from very cheap paperback editions, to very expensive leather-bound gilt-edged editions. If they have none, or if they only have a kind you would not choose, you can contact Veritas or the National Bible Society of Ireland.

2 ***You can start reading*** anywhere you like. A good place may be something direct and personal. For example, you could try St Mark's Gospel (the shortest); or St Paul's very personal letter to the Philippians; or sample some of the Psalms and see which speak for you; or the beautiful love story in the short Book of Ruth. Just ask yourself: *'Who is this person I'm reading about? How does this person experience God in his or her life? What does it say about my life?'* If you find that you stop reading after a short while, and find yourself almost praying (and finding it good!): don't be too

surprised! The reason for the Bible is for us to know God, and his son Jesus Christ. The Holy Spirit is with us to guide us.

3 ***You're not alone.*** The Word of God is for all of God's people. There are many other people who are on the same journey as you with the Bible. If you contact a local group, they may be following a plan of reading in which you could join and share discussion, as well as doing your own reading. The National Bible Society has some leaflets you may find a help: a ***Bible Reading Plan*** and ***Where to look in the Bible.*** There are also many books and booklets to help you. Once you begin to make it part of your regular 'diet', we hope you'll begin to think: *'Why on earth did I ever leave it so long!'*

APPENDIX 5

MARRIAGE AND NULLITY IN THE CATHOLIC CHURCH

Since this book looks particularly at preparing for a church wedding, you will hardly be surprised that it focuses principally on the positive and ideal understanding of marriage (while acknowledging that there are difficulties in every marriage). It would be strange if it were otherwise!

We know that life is not ideal. Each couple's experience of marriage is different. It may seem strange to deal with this in a book intended to do everything possible to promote fully developed lifelong relationships in Christian marriage! But because it is a topic about which there is some confusion, and because marriage 'breakdown' is well known, these few notes may be of assistance. Anyone wanting further information will need to look further afield for fuller treatment of the subject.

There can be many causes for marriage breakdown. Sometimes there may seem to be a total impossibility of continuing with the marriage, for many possible reasons. A relationship marked by violence, whether physical, emotional, sexual, or mental, is a shattering experience. Sometimes breakdown may arise due to the human weakness of one or other person in the marriage. In a time of some difficulty in the relationship (a normal experience), there may arise the temptation to find a way out through an offer of affection elsewhere. The normal development of mid-life can find a person abandoning a marriage of many years, which can be totally incomprehensible to all the friends of the couple. Whatever the situation, people can turn to their Church to see whether something can be done: whether a Decree of Nullity can be given in their case.

A decree of nullity means an authoritative declaration that a couple who at first seemed to be validly married never were in reality husband and wife. Our human experience is that not every married relationship proves happy or stable for a lifetime. This is not in itself evidence of nullity. Counselling and support can at times contribute a great deal to bring new hope and life. If these fail, what can be done? Is nullity really a kind of divorce under a different name to get the Church out of a difficulty?

Nullity is in fact something quite different. Divorce says: 'There was a marriage, and now we are declaring that it is finished'. Nullity says: 'What appeared to be a valid marriage is now seen not ever to have been so, for certain definite reasons'. There may be some impediment which means the marriage was not valid; or the marriage may not have been properly effected legally; or the consent may have been defective – one or both partners may not have given valid consent, or may have been incapable of carrying out what he or she undertook. A declaration of nullity, when eventually obtained, does not purport to claim that there was never any relationship, nor indeed, children. It does claim that from the evidence available now, that relationship was not a marriage. Any children of such a relationship are considered legitimate in Church law.

Here is not the place to deal further with the factors involved; what I wish to do is to give the overall Church approach to this matter. What I say here about the Church may not, unfortunately, be your experience of the Church, but it does reflect what we, the Church, are called to be, and what we try with God's help to be.

The Church is a group of people who recognise and accept the love that God has freely given us through his son, Jesus Christ. We, the followers of Jesus, are called to live a life of love for one another –

both friends and enemies. In loving one another, we come to recognise that we are experiencing the very love of God.

When two Christians marry, they are called to, and accept, the challenge of being a very special embodiment of God's unconditional, free and eternal love for us, in the way that they decide to love each other unconditionally for the rest of their married life. In accepting this vocation, they are a gift to the rest of us who are called to be the loving community of the Church, and to the world at large; and they call on us who are the Church to support them in living out their decision. Their decision is not a private one between themselves alone; it is a solemn covenant with the Church and with God. You'll find more about this in Part I of this book: 'Introducing Christian Marriage'.

When a marriage between Christians runs into difficulties that seem insoluble, they may decide to separate, but they are still committed to being faithful to each other. For a separated husband or wife to remain faithful, even if the other partner does not do so, is a witness to God's faithfulness to us even when we are unfaithful.

When a member of the Church asks to have the marriage looked at by the Church with a view to deciding whether it was ever a valid marriage or not, he or she is asking the community of love to decide on the situation insofar as it can be humanly assessed. The normal presumption is in favour of the validity of the marriage: we normally presume that people know what they are doing, and are capable of carrying out what they undertake. In order to overthrow such a presumption, concrete evidence is required, and this, in some cases, may simply not be available. The Marriage Tribunal, which is the body entrusted in a diocese or region with this aspect of the life of members of the Christian community, works with the available evidence. The status or wealth of the couple in question is not relevant to the outcome.

In cases where the marriage is not proven to be invalid, the partners in the marriage continue to be husband and wife, even if living apart; we need to have considerable support systems in the Church for those who are trying to live their vocation in a broken situation.

In cases where the marriage is proven to be invalid, the partners are seen by the community of the Church never to have been married in reality, although at first this seemed to be the case. Both parties in this situation are therefore free to marry since they are not in fact married; in many cases, however, a *vetitum* (a Latin word meaning 'prohibition') is applied. This means that one or both parties may not marry until it is clarified that whatever was the cause of the invalidity in the first case no longer exists. This is for the protection of all involved, so that another similar situation, with all the hurt involved, is, as far as is possible, avoided.

No human system or organisation is perfect. We know that the administration of justice in any country is imperfect. A man in the legal profession told me many years ago that when he was starting out, a more experienced person in the profession said to him: 'The courts are not there to provide justice. They are there to give people a chance to get justice'. So what happens if a Church Marriage Tribunal, after full consideration, does not see its way to granting a Decree of Nullity, and the couple are still husband and wife in the eyes of the Church? There seems to be no perfect answer here.

What if people then enter a second relationship, perhaps following a civil divorce? While being faithful to the Christian understanding of marriage, to judge harshly or to condemn those who honestly do not seem to find it within themselves to share and live by the ideals of Christian marriage is not the way of Christian love. Some people protest at what they see as the unjustified harshness of their Church. Perhaps in the future we may find better ways of coping with these situations; perhaps it is simply part of the fabric of human life, the human condition. I do not have an answer here. Perhaps I may just quote what Pope John Paul II said in January 1997: 'Let these men and women know that the Church loves them, that she is not far from them, and suffers because of their situation'. We need to find ways to ensure that this will be the experience of people in this situation, keeping in mind that to say that 'the Church loves them' must mean that we, you and I and the other members of the community of the Church at all levels, love them. We as a Church must do all we can to welcome those whose marriage situation does not reflect the ideal of Christian marriage in some way, and to encourage them to be as fully active as members of their local church as is possible.

All this is very general. Any married couple in difficulty is entitled to all the support we, the Church, can give. Only in the special circumstances of each couple can this be done. Your Church in your parish and diocese is at your service with as much love as can humanly be given.

A lot more could, of course, be said. This is just a brief look at the situation, so as to underline how important a gift each individual is in the Church, and how important a gift marriage is. Each individual marriage is of unbelievable value, and the people involved need all our gentleness and love and understanding so that they can grow to the fullness of their calling.

APPENDIX 6

EASTER DATES IN THE 21ST CENTURY

You want to plan your wedding date at a time that is good both for you and for the Church community. Most of the year, there is no problem. However, you will appreciate that Holy Week – the week before Easter – is not a good time to arrange a wedding. Lent too, from Ash Wednesday to Holy Week, is a time of penance to prepare for Easter. We recommend also not to celebrate your wedding in the weeks of Lent, if possible.

The date of Easter varies according to the natural cycles of earth, sun and moon, according to the Jewish tradition of celebrating Passover, which was the time of the death and resurrection of Jesus. Easter is celebrated on the first Sunday following the first full moon after the Spring equinox of the northern hemisphere (the Autumn or Fall equinox of the southern hemisphere). This equinox (21 or 22 March) is half-way between mid-winter and mid-summer. A full moon recurs about every twenty-nine days; a year is about 365 days. Orthodox Churches which follow a different calendar sometimes coincide, but often have their Easter celebration on a different day.

The earliest that Easter can fall in our calendar is 22 March; the latest is 25 April. See 2008 and 2038 for the earliest and latest in this century. (We have to wait until 2285 for Easter to be on 22 March!)

Ash Wednesday is the start of **Lent**, which has six Sundays, and finishes on Holy Thursday evening, the Thursday before Easter Sunday, at the start of the Easter Triduum, or the Three Great Days. The Easter Season finishes at **Pentecost Sunday** (also called 'Whit Sunday'), fifty days (seven weeks) after Easter, when we celebrate the coming of the Holy Spirit. Being a time of special celebration, this is a good time, as is most of the year.

Year	**Ashes**	**Easter**	**Pentecost**
2001	28 Feb	15 April	3 June
2002	13 Feb	31 March	19 May
2003	5 March	20 April	8 June
2004	25 Feb	11 April	30 May
2005	9 Feb	27 March	15 May
2006	1 March	16 April	4 June
2007	21 Feb	8 April	27 May
2008	6 Feb	23 March	11 May
2009	25 Feb	12 April	31 May
2010	17 Feb	4 April	23 May
2011	9 Mar	24 April	12 June
2012	22 Feb	8 April	27 May
2013	13 Feb	31 March	19 May
2014	5 March	20 April	8 June
2015	18 Feb	5 April	24 May
2016	10 Feb	27 March	15 May
2017	1 March	16 April	4 June
2018	14 Feb	1 April	20 May
2019	6 March	21 April	9 June
2020	26 Feb	12 April	31 May
2021	17 Feb	4 April	23 May
2022	2 March	17 April	5 June
2023	22 Feb	9 April	28 May
2024	14 Feb	31 March	19 May
2025	5 March	20 April	8 June
2026	18 Feb	5 April	24 May

Year	Ashes	Easter	Pentecost
2027	10 Feb	28 March	16 May
2028	1 March	16 April	4 June
2029	14 Feb	1 April	20 May
2030	6 March	21 April	9 June
2031	26 Feb	13 April	1 June
2032	11 Feb	28 March	16 May
2033	2 March	17 April	5 June
2034	22 Feb	9 April	28 May
2035	7 Feb	25 March	13 May
2036	27 Feb	13 April	1 June
2037	18 Feb	5 April	24 May
2038	10 March	25 April	13 June
2039	23 Feb	10 April	29 May
2040	15 Feb	1 April	20 May
2041	6 March	21 April	9 June
2042	19 Feb	6 April	25 May
2043	11 Feb	29 March	17 May
2044	2 March	17 April	5 June
2045	22 Feb	9 April	28 May
2046	7 Feb	25 March	13 May
2047	27 Feb	14 April	2 June
2048	19 Feb	5 April	24 May
2049	3 March	18 April	6 June
2050	23 Feb	10 April	29 May
2051	15 Feb	2 April	21 May
2052	6 March	21 April	9 June
2053	19 Feb	6 April	25 May
2054	11 Feb	29 March	17 May
2055	3 March	18 April	6 June
2056	16 Feb	2 April	21 May
2057	7 March	22 April	10 June
2058	27 Feb	14 April	2 June
2059	12 Feb	30 March	18 May
2060	3 March	18 April	6 June

Year	Ashes	Easter	Pentecost
2061	23 Feb	10 April	29 May
2062	8 Feb	26 March	14 May
2063	28 Feb	15 April	3 June
2064	20 Feb	6 April	25 May
2065	11 Feb	29 March	17 May
2066	24 Feb	11 April	30 May
2067	16 Feb	3 April	22 May
2068	7 March	22 April	10 June
2069	27 Feb	14 April	2 June
2070	12 Feb	30 March	18 May
2071	4 March	19 April	7 June
2072	24 Feb	10 April	29 May
2073	8 Feb	26 March	14 May
2074	28 Feb	15 April	3 June
2075	20 Feb	7 April	26 May
2076	4 March	19 April	7 June
2077	24 Feb	11 April	30 May
2078	16 Feb	3 April	22 May
2079	8 March	23 April	11 June
2080	21 Feb	7 April	26 May
2081	12 Feb	30 March	18 May
2082	4 March	19 April	7 June
2083	17 Feb	4 April	23 May
2084	9 Feb	26 March	14 May
2085	28 Feb	15 April	3 June
2086	13 Feb	31 March	19 May
2087	5 March	20 April	8 June
2088	25 Feb	11 April	30 May
2089	16 Feb	3 April	22 May
2090	1 March	16 April	4 June
2091	21 Feb	8 April	27 May
2092	13 Feb	30 March	18 May

APPENDIX 7

WEDDING CHECKLIST

This list is to make it easy for you to check relevant items. You may decide to omit some of these yourselves; the list is to make sure you don't leave out something you would like to arrange. The number in brackets before an item is the page number where that topic starts.

BEFOREHAND

(21) Contact your two parishes at least three months before
(22) Notify civil registrar at least three months before
(21) Marriage preparation course
(21) Book church
(21) Confirm availability of priest or other minister
(19) Wedding Ceremony or Wedding Mass
(21) Marriage papers
(81) Plan ceremony *(see elements of the ceremony below)*
(89) Music programme confirmed
(70) Personal preparation
(74) Papal Blessing
(75) Various items:

(67) Invitations to the wedding
(67) Reception decisions
(75) Passports
(75) Money matters
(77) Photographer, etc.

The Ceremony

People

(87) Witnesses
(87) Priest/deacon/minister
(87) Greeters/ushers/commentator
(87) Altar servers
(89) Music leader(s)
(88) Readers for Scripture readings (also p. 106)
(88) Readers for General Intercessions (Prayer of the Faithful)
(89) Minister(s) of the Eucharist
(78) Artwork: flowers, décor, etc.
(88) Preparation of gifts (& altar)

Elements of the Ceremony (not all elements may apply)

Introductory Rites:

(101)	Reception of the couple	
(101)	Entrance Music *or* Antiphon	Music *or* A B C
(102)	Greeting	A B C
(102)	Penitential Rite	A B C
(103)	Gloria	
(104)	Opening Prayer	A B C D

Liturgy of the Word:

(111)	Old Testament	1 2 3 4 5 6 7 8 9 *other*
(126)	Psalm	1 2 3 4 5 6 7 *other*
(132)	New Testament	1 2 3 4 5 6 7 8 9 10 11 12 13 14 *other*
(152)	Gospel Acclamation	1 2 3 4 *other*
(154)	Gospel	1 2 3 4 5 6 7 8 9 10 *other*

Rite of Marriage:
(See Appendix 3 for Rite for Scotland, England & Wales)

(168)	Address and Questions to the couple	1 2 3
(170)	Exchange of Consent	1 2 3 4
(173)	Blessing of ring(s)	1 2 3 4
(174)	Exchange of gifts	
(174)	Prayer of the couple	
(180)	GeneralIntercessions	
(175)	*or* Gnás an Phósta	

Liturgy of the Eucharist:

(183)	Preparation of the gifts and altar	
(185)	Prayer over gifts	1 2 3
(186)	Preface	1 2 3
(189)	Eucharistic Prayer	1 2 3 4 *or other*
(201)	Memorial Acclamation (Mystery of Faith)	1 2 3 4
(202)	Communion Rite	
(202)	The Lord's Prayer	English Irish
(203)	Nuptial Blessing	1 2 3 4 Irish
(210)	Sign of Peace	
(211)	Breaking of Bread	
(211)	Communion	Music *or* Antiphon 1 2 3
(212)	Prayer after Communion	1 2 3

Concluding Rite:

(213) Solemn Blessing 1 2 3 Irish

(216) Sending forth

(213) Signing of Civil Register (also p. 216)

Other notes: